PLACE VALUE

Place Value

An Educator's Guide to Good Literature on Rural Lifeways, Environments, and Purposes of Education

By
Toni Haas
and
Paul Nachtigal

Clearinghouse on Rural Education and Small Schools
Charleston, West Virginia

Clearinghouse on Rural Education and Small Schools
Appalachia Educational Laboratory
P.O. Box 1348, Charleston, WV 25325
www.ael.org/eric/

Printed by Chapman Printing Co., Huntington, WV
Cover illustration by John MacDonald, Williamstown, MA
Cover design by Richard Hendel, Chapel Hill, NC

Second Printing July 1999

Library of Congress Cataloging-in-Publication Data

Haas, Toni, 1942-
    Place Value: an educator's guide to good litereature on rural lifeways, environments, and purposes of education/by Toni Haas and Paul Nachtigal.
        p. cm.
    Includes bibliographical references (p.) and index.
    ISBN 1-880785-19-6 (paperback: alk. paper)
        1. Education—Aims and objectives—United States. 2. Education, Rural—United States. 3. Country life—Study and teaching—United States. 4. Politics and education—United States. 5. Education—Social aspects—Unites States. I. Nachtigal, Paul M. II. Title.
Z5815.U5H22   1998
[LA210]
016.37011'72'0973--dc21   99-21364
                                                                CIP

This publication was prepared with funding from the U.S. Department of Education, Office of Educational Research and Improvement, National Library of Education, under contract no. RR93002012. The opinions expressed herein do not necessarily reflect the positions or policies of the Appalachia Educational Laboratory, or the Department of Education.

The ERIC Clearinghouse on Rural Education and Small Schools is operated by the Appalachia Educational Laboratory (AEL), Inc. AEL is an Equal Opportunity/Affirmative Action Employer.

Table of Contents

Preface

What is the good life—material possessions, career success, personal wealth? How many people would trade the good life for deeper bonds with family, friends, and the world around them? *Place Value* looks at what it takes to enhance these connections, or live well, and how this wisdom can be imparted from one generation to another. It is written for people who wish to live well themselves and would like to help young people live well in a particular place

The philosophy of *living well* is most closely associated with the American rural way of life, a life characterized by production and sufficiency. Under attack from an array of outside economic and environmental forces, traditional rural life is rapidly vanishing as the chase for *the good life* depletes community after community. For the past century, the message about the good life has been clear: if you want good salaries, fine homes, and the world of mass culture, move to the city or suburbs. Rural schools have unwittingly contributed to this process. They educate students to take their places anywhere in the global economy and ignore the fact that *anywhere* usually means *elsewhere*. As the saying goes, rural young people graduate with a diploma in one hand and a bus ticket in the other.

Place Value challenges teachers to reexamine the purposes of education. On the dawn of the twenty-first century, our country tends to measure educational success by individual profit. We have forgotten that the top priority of schools is to serve the public good. What do students need to know about living well in their own communities? How does this affect them in the present and future? The answers may hold the solutions to rural America's dilemma.

Living well depends on the connections people have with one another and their surroundings. It is a conscious choice, not a matter of happenstance, genetics, or economic class. Protecting self-determination means equipping rural students and the adults who surround them with tools to create a different, better future. *Place Value* demonstrates ways in which teachers can relate their work and lives to the places where they live and help students do the same.

Place Value offers a variety of perspectives on what we think it means to live well in a particular place. Bibliographical essays describe some of the best available nonfictional and fictional literature on ecology, politics, economy, values, and spirituality—the themes we consider most essential to living well in rural places. An annotated bibliography with abstracts written especially for this volume or adapted from the ERIC database is also included to provide greater detail of the works cited.

We invite readers to disagree with our choices and create their own list of resources. Please communicate with the Clearinghouse or with us directly at The Rural Challenge, Box 1569, Granby, CO 80046.

Essay 1

A Sense of Place:
Education for Living Well Ecologically

All education is environmental education. By what is included or excluded, students are taught that they are part of or apart from the natural world.[1]

One of the most disingenuous proposals swirling around the push for national standards is the establishment of a national curriculum. In truth, a national curriculum has existed since the introduction of *McGuffey's Reader*. Textbook publishing is big business. Textbooks are written generically to appeal to the largest possible market. They must be inoffensive and useable in all parts of the country, particularly in large states such as California and Texas, which adopt them statewide. Curriculum is bound by what is in these textbooks. Standardized tests form the third leg of the iron triangle of the national curriculum.

What does this mean to students? Paul Gruchow writes

> Among my science courses I took two full years of biology, but I never learned that the beautiful meadow at the bottom of my family's pasture was a remnant virgin prairie. We did not spend, so far as I can remember, a single hour on the prairies—the landscape in which we were immersed—in two years of biological study.

> I took history courses for years, but I never learned that one of the founders of my town and for decades the leading banker . . . was also the author of the first comprehensive treatise on Minnesota's prairie

botany. I can only imagine now what it might have meant to me—a studious boy with a love of nature—to know that a great scholar of natural history had made a full and satisfying life in my town. I did not know until long after I left the place that it afforded the possibility of an intellectual life.

Nothing in my education prepared me to believe, or encouraged me to expect, that there was any reason to be interested in my own place. If I hoped to amount to anything, I understood, I had better take the first road east out of town as fast as I could. And, like so many of my classmates, I did.[2]

Gruchow was taught that he was separate from where he lived. An increasingly common theme for environmental philosophers is the re-examination of our relationship with the natural environment. Kirkpatrick Sale quotes Lewis Thomas:

Our deepest folly is the notion that we are in charge of the place, that we own it and can somehow run it. We are beginning to treat the earth as a sort of domesticated household pet, living in an environment invented by us, part kitchen garden, part zoo. It is an idea we must rid ourselves of soon, for it is not so. It is the other way around. We are not separate beings. We are a living part of the earth's life, owned and operated by the earth, probably specialized for functions on its behalf that we have not yet glimpsed.[3]

"Living part of the earth's life" means young people should be encouraged in their curiosity about their surroundings. There are wonderful examples of schools where the local place is becoming the curriculum. In northwestern Colorado, the Yampa Valley Legacy Education Initiative brings students from five small schools together to use the valley as a focus of study. The work is based on the belief that a careful study of one's own habitat reveals truths about the entire planet. Students are studying the history of the area from the earliest American Indian migrations while preserving the banks of one of the last free-flowing rivers in the country. They have created information kiosks that tell the river's story; tested water; charted fish, birds, and other wildlife; and compiled the results of their work at an information center. Perhaps most importantly, they are deeply involved in negotiations among ranching, mining, and tourist-industry interests. By attending public meetings, recording opinions, and articulating options, the students are learning mediation and group-process skills. The schools' goal is to help young people become stewards, rather than owners, of their valley.

Across the country, the Selborne Project in northern Pennsylvania and western New York is working with the Roger Tory Peterson Institute to create a place-based curriculum that focuses on a square kilometer of land adjacent to the school. Middle schoolers are learning the history, ecology, and social and physical infrastructure that surrounds them.

These and many other instances are teaching young people to become inhabitants, not residents, of their places. David Orr, in *Ecological Literacy,* explains the differences:

> The study of place . . . has a significance in reeducating people in the art of living well where they are. The distinction between inhabiting and residing . . . is important here. A resident is a temporary occupant, putting down few roots and investing little, knowing little, and perhaps caring little for the immediate locale beyond its ability to gratify. As both a cause and effect of displacement, the resident lives in an indoor world of office building, shopping mall, automobile, apartment, and suburban house and watches as much as four hours of television each day. The inhabitant, in contrast, "dwells," as Illich puts it in an intimate, organic, and mutually nurturing relationship with a place. Good inhabitance is an art requiring detailed knowledge of a place, the capacity for observation, and a sense of care and rootedness. Residence requires cash and a map. A resident can reside almost anywhere that provides an income. Inhabitants bear the marks of their places whether rural or urban, in patterns of speech, through dress and behavior. Uprooted, they get homesick. Historically, inhabitants are less likely to vandalize their or others' places. They also tend to make good neighbors and honest citizens. They are, in short, the bedrock of the stable community and neighborhood that Mumford, Dewey, and Jefferson regarded as the essential ingredient of democracy.[4]

And when a sense of place is missing? Wallace Stegner wrote about his feeling of disenfranchisement in *Wolf Willow:*

> I . . . read whatever books I could lay hands on, and almost everything I got from books was either at odds with what I knew from experience or irrelevant to it or remote from it. Books didn't enlarge me; they dispersed me. . . . The information I was gaining from literature and from books on geography and history had not the slightest relevance to the geography, history, or life of the place where I lived. Living in the Cypress Hills, I did not even know I lived there, and hadn't the faintest notion of who had lived there before me. In general the assumption of all of us, child or adult, was that this was a new country and that a new country had no history. History was something that happened to other

places. . . . So the world when I began to know it had neither location nor time, geography nor history.[5]

There are tight links between environment and community and between natural and human systems. Sustainable human systems cannot operate in ways incompatible with natural systems.

Just as there are natural laws—gravity being one—there are equally important laws that characterize sustainable communities. The survival of humanity depends on our understanding of how ecosystems organize themselves. Based on this, should local ecology not be a feature of education? Robert Bellah and his colleagues speak to this point in *The Good Society:*

> It is characteristic of that older form of knowing which Dewey located in the household and the neighborhood that one learns, not through accumulating tested propositions about the objective world, but through participation in social practices, by assuming social roles, by becoming familiar with exemplary narratives and with typical characters who illustrate a variety of patterns of behavior. One does not feel like an autonomous subject learning specific facts about an objective world out there. One becomes what one knows.[6]

We know, at a very deep level, that "landscape shapes mindscape."[7] Our first question to strangers is "Where are you from?" Our answers are geographic ("I'm from the South") or focus on natural features ("I live in the mountains"). Yet most of us are bone ignorant of the places we claim so proudly, and the fault lies with an education that has been systematically stripped of its context. The results are as barren as the landscapes they echo. Wendell Berry writes in *The Unsettling of America*

> We have given up the understanding—dropped it out of our language and so out of our thought—that we and our country create one another, depend on one another, are literally part of one another; that our land passes in and out of our bodies just as our bodies pass in and out of our land; that as we and our land are part of one another, so all who are living as neighbors here, human and plant and animal, are part of one another, and so cannot possibly flourish alone; that, therefore, our culture must be our response to our place, our culture and our place are images of each other and inseparable from each other, and so neither can be better than the other.[8]

In *Rooted in the Land*, William Vitek and Wes Jackson observe the bond rural people have with the places where they live:

doesn't always foster respect carrying mind of actions

The connection between human communities and place is not unique to rural areas, but here one can be certain that the land is not mere scenery and hiking trail, or resources in need of extraction. Here the land becomes part of people's lives, intermingled with buying and selling, working and playing, living and dying. It is both history and future. In rural communities is an opportunity for the land's rhythms to become part of everyday life, an immediate linkage between the land's fertility and the community's prosperity. . . . Here the wisdom of limitations accrues incrementally but forcefully in daily routines and practices informed by communal labor and natural rhythms. . . . At their best, working agricultural and rural landscapes provide insight into the types of communities, practices, virtues, and values that will facilitate the transition to an environmental ethos.[9]

In many rural communities, schools have become vehicles for educating people to leave, fulfilling the prophecy that these places are doomed to poverty, decline, and despair. They have cooked their own goose, just as Aldo Leopold predicted:

I once knew an educated lady, banded by Phi Beta Kappa, who told me that she had never heard or seen the geese that twice a year proclaim the revolving seasons to her well-insulated roof. Is education possibly a process of trading awareness for things of lesser worth? The goose who trades his is soon a pile of feathers.[10]

Awareness of local things disappears in the crush of standardized curricula, generic textbooks, and centralized test design. These practices are invented by and for an urban industrial age. Well-insulated roofs blocking the music of geese symbolize the insulated walls that shield classroom learning from applications in life.

John McPhee, nonfiction's most brilliant practitioner, writes about how the very earth under our feet was formed. We recommend, as a sampler, the *Second John McPhee Reader* as an introduction to this most basic of all mysteries.

Schools and school reform have too often become the enemy of living well ecologically. This kind of relationship is bad for children, schools, and rural communities. When schools are disconnected from specific places and life in communities, they cease to be public institutions, serving the public good. Alternatively, by developing a healthy respect for the physical and social communities they inhabit, schools can teach children to be contributing citizens, no matter where the students end up living their lives, earning their livings, and practicing democracy.

A Sense of Civic Involvement: Education for Living Well Politically

Dismay, distrust, and despair currently envelop the American political world, an indication of our inability to create coherent stories about our lives.[1] As public institutions charged with preparing young people to participate as citizens in the democracy, schools must help change these perceptions.

One hundred fifty years ago, Alexis de Tocqueville observed

> It cannot be doubted in the United States the instruction of the people powerfully contributes to the support of the democratic republic. . . . I am still further from thinking, as many people do think in Europe, that men can be instantaneously made citizens by teaching themselves to read and write. True information is mainly derived from experience; and if the Americans had not been gradually accustomed to govern themselves, their book-learning would not help them much in the present day.[2]

As Michael Sandel points out, grounding political education in a particular place is crucial:

> Since the days of Aristotle's *polis*, the republican tradition has viewed self-government as an activity rooted in a particular place, carried out by citizens loyal to that place and the way of life it embodies.[3]

Linked as we are to the global village, self-government must find its roots in a particular place. Helping students identify, investigate, and act on municipal and county government issues teaches principles of citizenship more meaningfully than abstract discussions of the three branches of a distant government. Students learn that the world begins locally but does not stop there. Sandel notes that more is required once this base is established:

> Self-government today, however, requires a politics that plays itself out in a multiplicity of settings, from neighborhoods to nations to the world as a whole. Such a politics requires citizens who can think and act as multiply-situated selves. The civic virtue distinctive to our time is the capacity to negotiate our way among the sometimes overlapping, sometimes conflicting obligations that claim us, and to live with the tension to which multiple loyalties give rise. This capacity is difficult to sustain, for it is easier to live with the plurality between persons than within them.
>
> The global media and markets that shape our lives beckon us to a world beyond boundaries and belonging. But the civic resources we need to master these forces, or at least to be content with them, are still to be found in the places and stories, memories and meanings, incidents and identities, that situate us in the world and give our lives their moral particularity.[4]

This strong civic base sets the stage for citizen action. Students in Howard, South Dakota, used *The Broken Heartland*[5] as a study guide, applying Osha Gray Davidson's research about the farm crisis in Iowa to their circumstances. One girl collected photographs documenting the history of her family's farm from the time it was homesteaded by her great-grandfather, through the purchase of larger and larger tractors by each generation, to the final auction of the land because her family could no longer pay the interest charges on their loans. The photos were set off by text, describing the place, time, and people, and the larger story was told using quotations from *The Broken Heartland*. One of her classmates uncovered that most presidential appointments to the Department of Agriculture had links to agribusiness and few had experience with family farms. She pointed this out in a letter to her senator and the president. Other teams of young people gathered comparable economic data in Miner County, created their own analysis for the county and state, and presented this data to their newly elected senator, Tim Johnson. As he told CNN, Johnson took their book to his office in the U.S. Capitol to "remind me why I'm here."

Sandel adds that telling a community's story is key to the survival of self-government:

> Corruption to which multiply-encumbered citizens are prone is the drift to formless, protean, storyless selves, unable to weave the various strands of their identity into a coherent whole. Political community depends on the narratives by which people make sense of their condition and interpret the common life they share; at its best, political deliberation is not only about competing policies but also about competing interpretations of the character of a community, its purposes and ends. There is a growing danger that, individually and collectively, we will find ourselves slipping into a fragmented, storyless condition. The loss of the capacity for narrative would amount to the ultimate disempowering of the human subject, for without narrative there is no continuity between present and past, and therefore no responsibility, and therefore no possibility of acting together to govern ourselves.[6]

Public support for public education is vested in the trust that the return on our investments (time, concern, and taxes) to educate other people's children transcends benefits to individuals. The fear of citizens that their trust has been misplaced is eroding support for public schools, even in rural America. David Mathews comments on this loss of faith:

> If the schools are losing the public, as the research suggests, or if "public" schools mean little more today than schools paid for by taxes and controlled by boards of citizens, then no plan for reform or reorganization should be attempted without looking at its impact on what appears to be a very fragile relationship. . . . Any arrangement that makes our schools less public will have serious consequences— not only for schools but for an entire country that was organized around the expectation that there would always be public education to "complete the great work of the American Revolution."[7]

And how do we "complete the great work of the American Revolution" in an era of globalization? Are we not grasses trampled by passing elephants? Sandel thinks not necessarily:

> In the age of NAFTA, the politics of neighborhood matters more, not less. People will not pledge allegiance to vast and distant entities, whatever their importance, unless those institutions are somehow connected to political arrangements that reflect the identity of the participants.[8]

Public schools shoulder responsibility as public institutions to help young people claim their identities as inhabitants of a particular place. When they turn eighteen, every student deserves a card from the superintendent of the local school, welcoming him or her to the noble ranks of voters. In preparation for that momentous event, young people should experience local and county government, research issues, sponsor candidate forums, and attend meetings as part of their course work. The school itself can be a living laboratory of democratic principles by providing rehearsals in civic practice.

Teachers should send students out to see for themselves how democracy works. Current practice asks young people to study government from a textbook, so they end up knowing more about Congress than about their state legislature or county government, which have stronger, more immediate impacts on their lives. A teacher in Del Norte, Colorado, requires her high school students to attend at least three meetings of public deliberative bodies each semester. Students must research what public deliberative bodies exist locally, choose one in which they are interested, and follow an issue to its conclusion. As a result, discussions of the issues have spilled out of the classroom into family conversations, often with the student as the authority; the earnestness and intensity of students in the audience (sometimes the only members of the public present) have changed the dynamics of the meetings and evoked inter-generational mutual respect; students have learned to identify and articulate local problems at a sophisticated level; and students have begun serving on committees and running for office.

Sandel believes every citizen should learn how to reinvigorate public life:

> The inability of the reigning political agenda to address the erosion of self-government and community reflects the impoverished conceptions of citizenship and freedom implicit in our public life.[9]

Benjamin R. Barber suggests every citizen should reexamine his or her public responsibility:

> Citizenship has lost its currency. It has come to mean little more than voting, when it means anything at all. Democratic politics has become something we watch rather than something we do.[10]

Supporting public education has come to mean little more than paying taxes. Even education professionals confuse public support with getting larger budgets. We need public schools to be public institutions, the centers of a reinvigorated public life.

Kettering Foundation research suggests that reinvigorating public life and living well politically require articulating the problem, inventing solutions, and finding others who will join you. Education in a democracy should create opportunities for young people to rehearse these steps.

Mathews mentions another way schools can foster a vibrant public life in their communities. Schools must simply welcome the public into their buildings:

> A public needs regular opportunities, occasions, meetings, or "space," to do its work; it also needs open channels of communication that are linked to crosscutting networks. Communities must have places where different people can talk about common problems—either formally, in town meetings or forums, or informally, in one-to-one or small-group conversations. These places are essential for generating political will, solving public problems and, most of all, creating citizens.

> Civil infrastructure rests on an informal social system. Festivals, Little League baseball games, soccer matches, neighborhood parties, and potluck dinners bring people together. More than social events, these gatherings help people form closer ties to their communities. . . . To strengthen public life . . . there have to be occasions where people can get to know one another as individuals. . . . Also people must have opportunities to engage in a larger conversation about the well-being of the community as a whole. And there have to be inclusive gatherings, inclusive with respect to who organizes them as well as who takes part in them. Citizens must be able to find others who have similar or related interests.[11]

Sounds like a rural school, right? At least it sounds like the rural school your parents or grandparents attended. Reclaiming this role of convening and providing space to the public serves the school well. It creates social capital that says education is important, relinks the public with the school, and builds community through civic action. This demonstrates to young people that civic involvement is part of being an American adult. Sandel reminds us that foundations of a republic "require public spaces that gather citizens together, enable them to interpret their condition, and cultivate solidarity and civic engagement."[12]

Rural schools can play several roles in helping rural people live well politically. The first is to create opportunities for young people to learn through practice their roles as citizens in a democracy. The second is to follow democratic principles and decision making in their operations. And the third is to nurture democratic deliberation by providing physical space, intellectual leadership, and fervent encouragement. The authors of *The Good Society* conclude public institutions need to rethink their responsibility to democracy:

> The great classic criteria of a good society—peace, prosperity, freedom, justice—all depend today on a new experiment in democracy, a newly extended and enhanced set of democratic institutions, within which we citizens can better discern what we really want and what we ought to want to sustain a good life on this planet for ourselves and the generations to come.[13]

The rural school is one of these extended and enhanced democratic institutions. The quality of all our lives depends on raising a generation of young people to take their places as participants in a moral, communal, and democratic society. Else, there will be no living well together, and we will have trashed the legacy of the American Revolution.

A Sense of Worth:
Education for Living Well Economically

I'd love to live in a small town or out in the country, where my family could know and be known by our neighbors, where my kids were safe, and where we could really belong and make a difference, but there's no way to make a living there.

Every survey that asks quality-of-life questions gets some variation of the response above. This widely held perception is the result of a hundred years of capitalism gone amok. Over the last century, rural America's population has dissipated as people have hastened to find jobs in urban factories. To reverse this trend, rural people should have better access to, and be taught to interpret economic information. Failing to do so continues the tradition Paul Gruchow describes:

Rural children have been educated to believe that opportunity of every kind lies elsewhere and that the last half century's rural experience of failure and decline has been largely due to the incompetence, or irrelevance, of rural people.[1]

For example, we need to help rural citizens—students and adults—understand the implications of giant global companies in this post-industrial age. *The Denver Post* discovered that many of these corporations have become bigger than the countries where they do business:

Mitsubishi is bigger than Indonesia, Ford is bigger than Turkey, and Wal-Mart is bigger than Israel, according to the Institute for Policy Studies. In fact, more than half of the 100 biggest economies in the world are corporations, not nations. Taken together, the world's 200 biggest companies control no less than 28 percent of the globe's economic activity.[2]

Dan Kemmis, former mayor of Missoula, Montana, explains why this matters:

> The problem of the role of corporations in public life helps to focus the larger problem of our declining capacity for being public at all. . . . We have lost so much of our sense of public identity. Corporations have always existed at public dispensation . . . only because the public thought it was going to get more than it would lose in the bargain. Corporations only become a problem . . . when the public loses its ability to enforce this bargain.[3]

Corporations are much more than manufacturing plants. They send tentacles well into the countryside. The top five percent of American landowners possess 75 percent of our land; the bottom 78 percent own just three percent. These remarkable numbers point out that family farms are not lost; they are collected by corporate owners. Davidson reminds us "on the eve of the revolution in Cuba, the largest nine percent of all landowners held 62 percent of that country's land, while 66 percent owned only seven percent."[4] The great American struggle has always been whether power and great wealth should be controlled by the many or the few. Davidson looks at the debate between Thomas Jefferson and Alexander Hamilton:

> Jefferson's allegiance to the yeoman farmer was based not so much on simple-minded agrarianism as it was on his belief that family farmers would form the cornerstone of a lasting American democracy because they (1) were economically and politically independent from a ruling elite, and (2) had a stake in the fortunes of the new country because they owned land. . . . Jefferson advocated dividing up the country's vast fertile lands into modest parcels and turning them over to small farmers at no charge. . . . Hamilton favored rule by "the rich and well-born." . . . He wanted federal land to be sold freely to the highest bidder, a policy which would benefit the federal treasury and land speculators the most.[5]

The human cost in the very real present is made visible both in fiction and nonfiction. Lest you think this is a Midwestern problem only, here is a range of books describing similar phenomena across the country.

The Grapes of Wrath by John Steinbeck is often on must-read lists for literature classes. Rich discussions result from comparing the Joad family saga with Jane Smiley's *A Thousand Acres*, which describes how today, in Iowa, a new migrant class is being created. A nonfiction account in Sam Bingham's *The Last Ranch* tells the story of ranching, public lands, and water issues in the Rocky Mountains. Victor Hanson's *Fields Without Dreams* reports from the perspective of a fifth-generation vine and fruit grower in California, and Steve Fisher's *Fighting Back in Appalachia: Traditions of Resistance and Change* moves the geography, but not the essence of the battle, to the eastern mountains.

The migration of rural people early in the century provided workers for urban factories. As the economy restructured, extractive industries (agriculture, mining, and lumber) substituted machinery for labor, employing fewer people. Mergers and acquisitions created markets with few sellers (oligopolies). Manufacturing located where it had cheap power (mill towns), cheap transportation (urban hubs for most of the first part of this century), and cheap labor (since the 1960s, primarily in the South to avoid unions and high taxes). With the emergence of multinational corporations and the search for the cheapest labor, manufacturing has moved to less developed nations.

Processing plants for meat and fish have produced the single exception to rural out-migration. These industries like to locate near their supplies in the country. Civic leaders welcome these new businesses and compete with other towns by offering tax breaks, guaranteeing loans, and promising little trouble from the local community. However, food-processing workers rarely earn a "living wage." They work for an average of nine dollars an hour in communities where local housing costs the equivalent of twelve dollars an hour.

Difficult, dangerous, and dirty, most packing-plant jobs do not go to local people. They are filled by imported workers in a conscious strategy to avoid unionization. Many of the new workers are single men between the ages of eighteen and twenty-four, statistically the most crime- and violence-prone group in any society. Poor working conditions, crowded housing, and limited opportunities for healthy off-hours' recreation lead to problems with law enforcement, causing resentment from local people. The community often picks up the tab for providing social services to workers with families, because employers ignore that responsibility. Tensions emerge as competition for resources pit one group of culturally distinct employees against another and all workers against the community. And plants recruit rural young people by advertising job opportunities in high school newspapers. These students should use books like *Any Way You Cut It: Meat*

Processing and Small Town America to understand their economy and alternatives for their community.

Understanding where we are and how we got there are only the first two steps. We also need to help young people understand how to create different futures for themselves. Rural schools should teach how to create jobs, not just how to get jobs working for someone else. Entrepreneurship education is vital to the survival of rural communities and can be offered as a community service to all citizens. Schools can provide the local resources for an economic renaissance by making available their facilities and equipment and working closely with state and local development agencies, extension agents, and community colleges.

Innovative rural schools hold classes in rural research and development, substituting real work in real time for abstract "contemporary-problems" curricula. These courses serve their communities, reinvigorate rigorous learning, and re-engage students turned off by more traditional approaches. Students have researched community needs for low-cost housing grants, conducted market-leakage studies to encourage local purchasing for chambers of commerce, and provided background information and guided tours to relocating firms. At the Coastal Studies Institute in Oregon, young people work as research scientists, gathering information on water quality and fish life under a contract with the Bureau of the Fisheries. Young entrepreneurs in Minnesota manage local groceries, lumber yards, and ice cream shops, all of which would have closed upon the retirement of the original owners. The REAL program, operating in fourteen states, integrates entrepreneurship education as an elective class in high schools and community colleges.

The economic future of rural America can no longer be left to market forces. History teaches us that those forces are neither neutral nor benign. Niche markets, local value-added production, and telecommunications that disseminate information everywhere are creating new jobs. Rural schools owe their students and communities access to these opportunities. We need to make our own economic future one that values place.

Essay 4

A Sense of Connection:
Education for Living Well Spiritually

not just american

While the legacy of American education is one of spectacular scientific and technological achievement . . . the cost has been inexorably high. American prosperity has come at the expense of the environment's degradation and has resulted in unprecedented exploitation of human and material resources worldwide. What underlies the crisis of American education is the crisis of modern man's identity and his cosmological disconnection from the natural world. Those who identify most with the bottom line often suffer from an image without substance, technique without soul, and knowledge without a context. Education is, at its essence, learning about life through participation and relationship in community, including not only people, but plants, animals, and the whole of Nature.[1]

There was a time when spirituality was not considered an appropriate subject for public schools, indeed for public discourse. It was a private matter examined in the context of particular religious faiths. We are coming to understand that living well includes this important, transcendent dimension.

Spirit is the foundation of indigenous knowledge, process, and religious expression. It also forms the ecological context through which to observe and integrate those understandings, bodies of knowledge, and practices resulting from direct interaction with the natural world. Gregory Cajete, whose words from *Look to the Mountain* open this essay, and Oscar

we've replaced w/ science

Kawagley, in *A Yupiaq World View*, give us profound insights into this ancient, integrated way of knowing what it means to live well.

In *Altars of Unhewn Stone*, Wes Jackson moves the discussion to science and the earth:

> Results are not guaranteed by simply increasing the volume of education without attending to the content as well. [We need] additional content to change our loyalties and affections.[2]

You will find this new content in books for every audience. Very young children respond to the chapter in Kenneth Grahame's *Wind in the Willows* called "Piper at the Gates of Dawn," where the exhausted Ratty and Mole are sheltered by the great Pan. Byrd Baylor's *I'm In Charge of Celebrations* and Douglas Wood's beautiful *Old Turtle* also reveal these close connections. Middle-grade children can easily read and talk about the ideas in Barry Lopez's *The Rediscovery of North America*. All of his books are wonderful. The Orion Society (136 East 64th Street, New York, NY 10021) has a fine bibliography of nature stories for children called *Bringing the World Alive*.

Linda Hasselstrom suggests you are never too young to develop spiritual links with the land:

> I wasn't born on the land; I was reborn here when I moved from a small city to a ranch at the age of nine. I was adopted by the land, and began developing a personal land ethic the first time I looked out on the empty, rolling prairie around my home.[3]

In everything she writes, Barbara Kingsolver rejoices in the spiritual connections between people and the nature of which they are a part. Teenagers in particular will enjoy her book of essays, *High Tide in Tucson*, which ties everyday life to its most fundamental context and brings wit to natural history.

Spiritual connections with nature are active, not passive. Kentucky philosopher, poet, and activist Wendell Berry writes forcefully about those connections. *The Unsettling of America* makes the case that agriculture is an integral part of the biological and cultural structure that sustains human life. In *The Gift of Good Land*, he challenges the interpretation of Genesis 1:28, in which Adam and Eve are instructed to "subdue" the earth. This passage has been used to justify the spiritual separation of people and the land and its creatures. Berry argues all living things are connected and demand mutual respect:

The divine mandate [is] to use the world justly and charitably . . . defin[ing] every person's moral predicament as that of a steward. . . . Stewardship is hopeless and meaningless unless it involves long-term courage, perseverance, devotion and skill. . . . The most necessary thing . . . is not to invent new technologies or methods, not to achieve "breakthroughs," but to determine what tools and methods are appropriate to specific people, places, and needs, and to apply them correctly. This is not to suggest that we can live harmlessly, or strictly at our own expense; we depend upon other creatures and survive by their deaths. To live, we must daily break the body and shed the blood of Creation. When we do this knowingly, lovingly, skillfully, reverently, it is a sacrament. When we do it ignorantly, greedily, clumsily, destructively, it is a desecration. In such desecration we condemn ourselves to spiritual and moral loneliness, and others to want.[4]

Spirituality and activism are linked as well in *Cold Anger: A Story of Faith and Power Politics*. Mary Beth Rogers recounts Ernesto Cortes's use of intellectualism, religious beliefs, and hardball politics to build a power base of local community organizations. Cortes's work is an example of the newly extended and enhanced set of democratic institutions called for by Bellah and his colleagues in *The Good Society*.

Many of the books in this essay are about agriculture, but that is not the only land in rural places. The unbroken land, or wilderness, is also important for spiritual connections. The not-for-profit press Milkweed Editions (430 First Avenue North, Suite 400, Minneapolis, MN 55401-1743) publishes books linking literature with a land ethic. The most recent example of their success is *Testimony: Writers of the West Speak on Behalf of Utah Wilderness*, which influenced passage of the Utah Wilderness legislation. In one of the essays, Karen Shepherd asserts the importance of nature:

Here [in the Wilderness], we can feel our spiritual connection to the earth challenging us to be better than we are, urging us to reach beyond where we have ever reached before. Here, we can imagine our beginnings and create possibilities for our future. . . . We must save wilderness because in saving it we will be saving part of ourselves. We have been shaped by the wild lands we have lived in, and because they are still part of our landscape, they continue to live within us. When they are gone, many of the fundamental values that created America will also vanish.[5]

ESSAY 5

A Sense of Belonging:
Education for Living Well in Community

If you want a better community, you will have to do the work yourself.[1]

Community is how we collectively create a story about our place. It is the narrative of who we are, how we get along together, how we make a living, and how we are connected. It is, Marty Strange says, about how we agree to continue to rub up against neighbors with whom we disagree. Community is how we live well together. In *The Good Society*, the authors discuss education's role in nurturing the collective good:

> On the whole, Americans have done better in developing their educational resources for the transmission of specialized knowledge and skills than they have for citizenship. . . . We must make changes... that show we understand education less obsessively in terms of "infrastructure for competition" and more as an invaluable resource in the search for the common good. Then we could realize how badly depleted our cultural endowment is throughout the educational process and cultivate again those resources without which reflection about a good society is impossible.[2]

Rural places in particular have depleted their cultural endowments. Wendell Berry recognizes that a community's collective memory is the key to survival:

A good local culture, in one of its most important functions, is a collection of the memories, ways, and skills necessary for the observance of preserving and improving the local soil. A human community, if it is to last long, must exert a sort of centripetal force, holding local soil and local memory in place. Practically speaking, human society has no work more important than this.[3]

Local memories, stories, and culture have been clear-cut no less than the forests. Rural people no longer want to be identified as rural, because it implies backward or ignorant with nothing of value to contribute to one another or to the larger society. They have internalized poisonous messages from the urban-dominated culture, and, as Berry observes, the problem runs even deeper:

> It would be somewhat more pleasant for country people if they could blame all this on city people. But the old opposition of country versus city . . . is far too simple to explain our problem. For country people more and more live like city people, and so connive in their own ruin. More and more country people, like city people, allow their economic and social standards to be set by television and salesmen and outside experts. As local community decays along with local economy, a vast amnesia settles over the countryside. As the exposed and disregarded soil departs with the rains, so local knowledge and local memory move away to the cities or are forgotten under the influence of homogenized sales talk, entertainment, and education. This loss of local knowledge and memory—that is, of local culture—has been ignored, or written off as one of the cheaper "prices of progress," or made the business of folklorists.[4]

Alan Peshkin writes insightfully about these links in *Growing Up American*. Paul Theobald's *Teaching the Commons: Place, Pride and the Renewal of Community* is a historical analysis of the notion of community. He teaches us about political choices that have erased people's ability to think and act for the commonweal. This is "must" reading in the populist tradition of learning for ourselves.

How do we stem this tide? One way is to learn from communities working to reclaim their cultures. Melissa Faye Greene tells the story of a Georgia community's awakening in *Praying for Sheetrock*, which relates McIntosh County's response to the civil rights movement in the 1970s. Abraham Verghese brings us up to the moment with *My Own Country: A Doctor's Story of a Town and Its People in the Age of AIDS*. Carol Stack's *Call to Home: African Americans Reclaim the Rural South* is about community-building going on right now.

Eliot Wigginton's *Sometimes a Shining Moment* provides practical, detailed advice for teachers:

> Students must have a firm understanding of the contemporary institutions that shape our lives. They must know the inner workings and ultimate purposes of our political systems—local, regional, and national—and how, why, and by whom those systems were set up and who runs them now. They must have an understanding of themselves as members of a society with a history and a future—they must understand how social groups function both in isolation from and in contact with others, and how such interactions can work in both positive and negative ways. . . . In short, we and our students must understand how the world works. The first step is to back up and examine our methodology and our review of what clearly works and what doesn't. As students acquire certain fundamentals and skills, our role may then become to help them put those skills to work in real ways. Skillful teachers find ways to give children reasons to communicate to real audiences.[5]

Wigginton's students found "local memories, knowledge, and skills" through interviews with local people. Collecting that important local culture, they created a publishing empire that involved records, tapes, films, a Broadway play, and more than twenty books. You and your students can find niches where you live, needs in your communities that are real and should be addressed.

In Alabama, as in many other places, most small towns no longer have a local newspaper. Only the county seat publishes a regular paper, generally providing communities with just an occasional column in which to comment on the history they are creating. The PACERS Cooperative, an association of almost thirty small schools, is supporting community/school newspapers published by students in more than a dozen small towns.

In Belle Fourche, South Dakota, the local paper hires journalism class members as "stringers." Their news stories are published as the official record in the weekly paper. Many schools have sponsored oral histories, uniquely valuable in themselves and training grounds for a renaissance in regional studies and writing rooted in place. We want students to learn that writing is thinking made visible, and it has consequences. Presenting one's work to a public audience brings those consequences home.

It is not just a matter for older students. Cynthia Parsons, author of *Serving to Learn, Learning to Serve: Civics and Service A to Z*, required her sixth-grade students to invent a community service, do it, and report to the class in two weeks. Discovering for oneself what community is and needs could move service learning out of the "make-work" category. Many projects called service learning actually involve repetitive tasks that adults would rather not do, such as picking up trash for the second or third time.

Wigginton was challenged to develop projects that met several goals at once by

> Teaching basic skills and life survival skills, showing how the world works, fostering involvement in and appreciation for the arts, building personal traits such as curiosity, self-confidence, independence, and self-esteem, and simultaneously moving the student beyond self into a caring relationship with humanity and the environment and a sense of the interdependence of all life—a big job indeed . . . the job of everyone from whom young people gain knowledge. It is for this reason that the best teachers, realizing the limitations on their time and energy, make sure that all the projects and lessons that take place in their classes serve double and triple functions; and they constantly strive to find activities that are so compelling and so rich that they go even beyond that. They are, in short, activities that serve nearly all the goals simultaneously, with no real increase in the time and energy required. . . . Suddenly rather than being narrow and pinched, they see things whole.[6]

Sometimes a Shining Moment is still the best book for high school teachers who feel caught between how they want to teach and what they are being told to teach. Ruth Charney, in *Teaching Children to Care*, describes how she works with elementary students to create a community-building classroom of young people who understand their links to one another and their contribution to the whole.

It is also in "seeing things whole" that leadership moves and has its being. Valuing place, connecting schools to communities in reciprocal relationships, and emphasizing the importance of learning to live well in community requires rare courage and self-confidence. These are activities that, in the beginning, need to be explained to the community, because they "don't look like school." Administrators in schools that value place are not only strong instructional leaders, they demonstrate a high level of trust in their faculty. They see the school and community boundaries as one, and the entire community becomes a laboratory for learning. They act as a moderator for the ongoing conversation among community leaders, school patrons, students, parents, and professional educators.

Some principals in rural communities relocate their offices for at least part of the day and go where people congregate to talk. They make themselves accessible by having coffee downtown, so people who do not want to make the trip to the school know where to find them when something "needs talked about." In doing so, they encourage the community to deliberate the purposes of education.

They make sure the school is open physically to serve the community. In cold climates, district residents are encouraged to take their daily walks in the school while the principal accompanies them, pointing out students' work and where help would be useful. A district in Kansas rents space to the U.S. Postal Service, ensuring that teachers see every resident every day. Using schools as polling places not only makes the buildings less mysterious, it teaches students lessons about democracy.

Rural principals need to open the schools psychologically as well, removing barriers and roadblocks to education. This demands changing restrictive schedules, state regulations, and traditional thinking of the faculty, staff, and community. Jim Lentz, a superintendent and former principal in Howard, South Dakota, describes the relationship between his community and school as a marriage in which each partner supports the other to grow and sees their fates intertwined. That metaphor became the core of their self-study for the North Central evaluation.

It is not as difficult as you may think to find others who believe valuing place is the answer to reforming education and life in rural America. Begin by reading some or all of the books recommended here (the bibliography will help you choose where to start). Talk with colleagues about this essay and the books you read. Use the Internet to find Web sites and connections to other people working on issues of place, community, and education reform. The Rural Challenge website is www.ruralchallenge.org; the group in Alabama working on environmentally sensitive entrepreneurial activities, documenting local history, publishing community/school newspapers, and sponsoring celebrations has a site at www.pacers.org. The ERIC Clearinghouse on Rural Education and Small Schools has a number of free and low-cost publications that examine the purposes of rural education and ways to sustain and keep small, rural schools (http://www.ael.org/eric/). You will surely find others.

See if you can begin a deliberation in your community on the local purposes of schooling. The Kettering Foundation sponsors National Issues Forums and has wonderful advice on how to get started. Write them at National Issues Forum, 100 Commons Road, Dayton OH 45459-2777 or call (800)433-7834.

This is where we are in our beliefs about the purposes of education and how we think schools can help us learn to live well. We can invent the world we want to live in by linking people and their places, reinvigorating an inclusive civic life, and creating economic opportunities that do not require us to leave home.

Endnotes

Essay 1. A Sense of Place: Education for Living Well Ecologically

1. David W. Orr, *Earth in Mind: On Education, Environment and the Human Prospect* (Washington, DC: Island Press, 1994), 130.

2. Paul Gruchow, *Grassroots: The Universe of Home* (Minneapolis: Milkweed Editions, 1995), 134-135.

3. Kirkpatrick Sale, *Dwellers in the Land: The Bioregional Vision* (San Francisco: Sierra Club Books, 1985; Philadelphia: New Society Publishers, 1991), 191-192.

4. David W. Orr, *Ecological Literacy: Education and the Transition to a Postmodern World* (Albany: State University of New York Press, 1992), 130.

5. Wallace Stegner, *Wolf Willow: A History, a Story, and a Memory of the Last Plains Frontier* (Lincoln: University of Nebraska Press, 1962), 26- 29. Penguin USA published a paperback edition in 1990.

6. Robert N. Bellah et al., *The Good Society* (New York: Knopf, 1991), 158. Vintage Books published a paperback edition in 1992.

7. Orr, *Ecological Literacy*, 6.

8. Berry, Wendell, *The Unsettling of America: Culture & Agriculture* (New York: Avon Books, 1977), 22. A more recent edition was published by Sierra Club Books in 1996.

9. William Vitek and Wes Jackson, eds., *Rooted in the Land: Essays on Community and Place* (New Haven: Yale University Press, 1996), 3.

10. Aldo Leopold, *A Sand County Almanac and Sketches Here and There: With Other Essays on Conservation from Round River* (New York: Oxford University Press, 1949, 1987), 18. Oxford University Press published a more recent edition in 1993.

Essay 2. A Sense of Civic Involvement: Education for Living Well Politically

1. The loss of faith in government was the dirty little secret unspoken in the 1996 election. It symbolizes the public's movement away from major institutions. From 1973 to 1993, the proportion of Americans who said they were confident in major institutions dropped alarmingly. Organized religion was down from 35 to 23 percent. Confidence in educational institutions dropped even farther, from 37 to 22 percent, and people who said they had little confidence in schools rose from 8 to 18 percent, according to the National Opinion Research Center, "Public Opinion and Demographic Report: Confidence in Institutions" *American Enterprise*, 4 (November 1993): 94-95.

2. Cynthia Parsons, *Serving to Learn, Learning to Serve: Civics and Service from A to Z* (Thousand Oaks, CA: Corwin Press, 1995), iv-v.

3. Michael J. Sandel, *Democracy's Discontent: America in Search of a Public Philosophy* (Cambridge, MA: Belknap Press of Harvard University Press, 1996), 349.

4. Ibid., 349-350.

5. Osha Gray Davidson, *Broken Heartland: The Rise of America's Rural Ghetto* (New York: Free Press, 1990; Iowa City: University of Iowa Press, 1996), 35.

6. Sandel, *Democracy's Discontent*, 351.

7. David Mathews, *Is There a Public for Public Schools?* (Dayton, OH: Kettering Foundation Press, 1996), 8. The Kettering Foundation published a paperback edition in 1997.

8. Sandel, *Democracy's Discontent*, 346.

9. Ibid., 323.

10. Benjamin R. Barber, *An Aristocracy for Everyone: The Politics of Education and the Future of America* (New York: Ballantine Books, 1992), 235. Oxford University Press published a paperback edition in 1994.

11. Mathews, *Is There a Public for Public Schools?*, 63-65.

12. Sandel, *Democracy's Discontent*, 349.

13. Bellah et al., *The Good Society*, 9.

Essay 3. A Sense of Worth: Education for Living Well Economically

1. Gruchow, *Grassroots*, 91.

2. R. C. Longworth, "Global Firms' Economic Power Boggling," *The Denver Post*, 13 October 1996.

3. Daniel Kemmis, *Community and the Politics of Place* (Norman: University of Oklahoma Press, 1990), 129. University of Oklahoma Press published a paperback edition in 1992.

4. Davidson, *Broken Heartland*, 35.

5. Ibid., 22-23.

Essay 4. A Sense of Connection: Education for Living Well Spiritually

1. Gregory Cajete, *Look to the Mountain: An Ecology of Indigenous Education* (Durango, CO: Kivaki Press, 1994), 25-26.

2. Wes Jackson, *Altars of Unhewn Stone: Science and the Earth* (San Francisco: North Point Press, 1987), 150.

3. Linda M. Hasselstrom, *Land Circle: Writings Collected from the Land* (Golden, CO: Fulcrum Publishing, 1991), 240. Fulcrum published a paperback edition in 1993.

4. Wendell Berry, *The Gift of Good Land: Further Essays, Cultural and Agricultural* (San Francisco: North Point Press, 1981), 272-281. North Point Press published a paperback edition in 1983.

5. Karen Shepherd, "Decision Time," in Stephen Trimble and Terry Tempest Williams, eds., *Testimony: Writers of the West Speak on Behalf of Utah Wilderness* (Minneapolis: Milkweed Editions, 1996), 24.

Essay 5. A Sense of Belonging: Education for Living Well in Community

1. Mathews, *Is There a Public for Public Schools?*, 69.

2. Bellah et al., *The Good Society*, 175.

3. Wendell Berry, *What Are People For?* (San Francisco: North Point Press, 1990), 154-155.

4. Ibid., 156-157.

5. Eliot Wigginton, *Sometimes a Shining Moment: The Foxfire Experience (Twenty Years Teaching in a High School Classroom)* (Garden City, NY: Anchor Books, 1985), 298-299.

6. Ibid., 301-320.

More About the Books:
An Annotated Bibliography

(organized by the order in which
works were cited in essays)

Each of the annotations in this section begins with comments by Haas and Nachtigal, followed by an abstract that describes the book in greater detail. Most of the abstracts have been adapted from document resumes first published in the ERIC Resources in Education database. A few were created especially for this volume. To avoid disclosing too much about their story lines, the works of fiction were not abstracted. Descriptions of those books include only the Haas and Nachtigal commentaries. —— Editor

A Sense of Place:
Education for Living Well Ecologically

Orr, David W. *Earth in Mind: On Education, Environment and the Human Prospect*. Washington, DC: Island Press, 1994.

We begin the first essay in this book with a quote from *Earth in Mind* because, more than any other book, it changed our minds. Orr makes a passionate case that educational reform is essential to reversing the rapid decline in the habitability of the earth. He illustrates how the human and economic forces that make communities stronger (or rip them apart) are connected with the very ground on which they stand. Here are fundamental answers to the question "What is education for?" What we need is "the capacity to understand the ecological context in which humans live, to recognize limits, and to get the scale of things right, changing the shape and dimension of our ideas and philosophies relative to the earth. The surest signs of ecological design intelligence are collective achievements: healthy, durable, resilient, just, and prosperous communities." This educator effectively lays out how to create experiences that help teachers and students develop such intelligence.

Abstract: This book, comprising 23 essays on the environmental crisis, argues that people are not taught to think broadly, to perceive systems and patterns, or to live as whole persons. Current educational reforms are driven by the belief that students must be prepared to compete in a global economy. A more important reason is the rapid decline in the habitability of the earth. Orr proposes that the disordering of the earth's ecological systems and great biogeochemical cycles reflects a prior disorder in the thought, perception, imagination, intellectual priorities, and loyalties inherent in the industrial mind. Ultimately, current ecological crises relate to how we think and the educational institutions that shape our capacity to think. Education should promote the development of ecological design intelligence, exemplified by healthy, durable, resilient, just, and prosperous communities. Part 1 addresses the purpose, dangers, and business of education. Part 2 suggests we rethink initial assumptions about learning and educational goals. As the curriculum has become more extensive, complex, and technologically sophisticated, we have lost the ability to ask questions about the human condition. Essays focus on love, intelligence, wisdom, virtue, responsibility, value, and good sense. Part 3 proposes new standards for educational quality to account for how institutions and their graduates affect the biotic world. Essays address institutional standards, disciplinary organization of learning, curriculum, professionalism, and implications of college architecture. Part 4 proposes an alternative destiny for education, exploring "biophilia," an innate affinity for life; obstacles to living well; and the future balance between rural and urban areas in a world that must come to grips with limits of many kinds.

Gruchow, Paul. *Grass Roots: The Universe of Home*. Minneapolis: Milkweed Editions, 1995.

Gruchow is a freelance writer and farm owner from Northfield, Minnesota. Like many of us, he grew up in a rural place and was persuaded by conventional wisdom he needed to leave that place to be "successful." He found, upon closer examination, that was not so. Gruchow's wonderfully crafted reflections on his pilgrimage provide a way for each of us to reexamine our fundamental values in this technological, consumer society. Using prairie metaphors, he challenges the injustices of our economic system, takes on the extractive nature of corporate food production, and analyzes education. The essay "What We Teach Rural Children" makes those of us who once taught in rural classrooms wish we could go back and correct some of our mistakes. *Grass Roots* helps us view the world through different lenses, think more clearly, and pay more attention to our particular place.

Abstract: This book consists of 17 essays about living with the land and the importance of reinvigorating the values of rural life. The essays include personal reflections on growing up in rural Minnesota and opinions about neglected rural towns and their people. Gruchow grew up during the 1950s on an 80-acre farm his family rented in Rosewood Township. They lived off the land. His father supplied the tools, labor, and seeds and kept two-thirds of the crop. Every summer, his mother canned vegetables, fruits, jams, sauces, and meats for the winter. Gruchow suggests the industrialization of farming has marginalized rural culture and impoverished rural towns and communities. Methods of acquiring bread demonstrate how industrialization has changed everyday life. When store-bought bread replaced home baking, the family abandoned more than a habit of living; they lost a piece of rural culture that affected their quality of life. Since 1910, industrialization has reduced the farm workforce from about fifty percent of the U.S. population to less than two percent and led to the development of a handful of huge, agribusiness corporations that dominate the American agricultural economy. Gruchow suggests we oppose any economic system that sees people as expendable resources, ignores the health of communities, and considers reductions in human labor as efficient. He questions the values rural people teach their children when, for the sake of a few jobs, they settle for the least attractive factory work and allow the rest of society to dump toxic trash on their land. Gruchow gives recommendations for education, agriculture, and economic development to reinvigorate rural communities and their way of life.

Sale, Kirkpatrick. *Dwellers in the Land: The Bioregional Vision.* San Francisco: Sierra Club Books, 1985; Philadelphia: New Society Publishers, 1991.

This book lays groundwork for the notion that the earth's biosphere is a system that exhibits the behavior of a single organism, even a living creature. The philosophy of bioregionalism nurtures and celebrates our local connections with the land; plants and animals; rivers, lakes, and oceans; air; families, friends, and neighbors; communities; native traditions; and systems of production and trade. This evolutionary movement embodies the virtue of gradualism, which mimics that of nature. Sale stimulates discussion on the movement, expressing the ideals of decentralism, participation, liberation, mutualism, and community. Presented with urgency and candor, this vision of scale, economy, polity, and society provides a clear alternative to the prevalent model.

Abstract: Bioregionalism has its roots in the Greek belief in Gaea, who represented the Earth and was worshiped as the universal mother. For many early societies, a belief in Gaea was synonymous with an environmental ethic of respect for the natural world and the sacredness of land. However, the evolution of a scientific worldview led to the abandonment of this ethic, resulting in the eradication of many societies. For example, the collapse of the Roman Empire can be attributed to the Romans' cumulative assaults on the Mediterranean ecology. Our ecology today is in greater danger than ever before. Sale argues we are using up natural resources faster than they can be replaced. To reverse this ecological disaster, the scientific worldview must be replaced with an ecological worldview. This bioregional philosophy focuses on the importance of region and community; advocates an economy based on conservation, stability, self-sufficiency, and cooperation; stresses a polity based on decentralization, complementarity, and diversity; and enables a society to understand the importance of symbiosis, evolution, and division. From an individual perspective, to become dwellers in the land requires knowing the land, learning the lore, developing the potential, and liberating the self.

Orr, David W. *Ecological Literacy: Education and the Transition to a Postmodern World.* Albany: State University of New York Press, 1992.

This book argues that all education is ecological education. Orr discusses how the earth's finiteness affects the content and substance of education. Given the limits of the earth, what should people know and how should they learn it? Central to Orr's thesis is the necessity of learning to live well in one's place. Formal education prepares graduates to reside, not dwell. For the resident, order begins from the top and proceeds downward as law and policy. For the inhabitant, order begins with the self and proceeds outward. His essay "Place and Pedagogy" provides a compelling rationale for making the study of place central to any curriculum. Knowing one's place provides the basis for building sustainable communities.

Abstract: These essays, written between 1984 and 1989, represent an extended reflection on the crisis of sustainability looming before the modern world and what this portends for the theory and practice of education. Part I helps clarify the concept and implications of sustainability. Essays in Part II analyze curriculum and pedagogy, asserting that the ecological crisis represents, in large measure, a failure of education. Reforming education is essential to solving the crisis described in Part I. Orr provides a list of 137 books as a "syllabus for ecological literacy." Essays in Part III are aimed at the pathologies of professionalized social science, targeting the Social Science Research Council, the U.S. Department of Agriculture, and those who presume the planet can be managed as if it were a giant corporation.

Stegner, Wallace. *Wolf Willow: A History, a Story, and a Memory of the Last Plains Frontier*. Lincoln: University of Nebraska Press, 1962; New York: Penguin USA, 1990.

This beautiful and moving book is a joy to read. It uniquely combines fiction and nonfiction, history and impressions, childhood remembrance, and adult reflection. Its language gives music and excitement to wisdom. Literature such as this is an integral part of "living well." Stegner was one of the premier writers about place. His place was the West. In another work, he challenged us to create a society to match the scenery. *Wolf Willow* helps us to think about place in general as we come to understand one particular location—the Cypress Hills country in southern Saskatchewan where Stegner's family homesteaded. "History is a Pontoon Bridge" eloquently critiques how literature ignores places like the Cypress Hills, making them invisible. Stegner spent a lifetime correcting that omission through his own writing and by encouraging other regional writers to raise their voices about forgotten places.

Bellah, Robert N., Richard Madsen, William M. Sullivan, Ann Swidler, and Steven M. Tipton. *The Good Society*. New York: Knopf, 1991; New York: Vintage Books, 1992.

The Good Society argues that understanding the common good comes from the shared understanding of the institutions through which we live.

We take responsibility for ourselves by taking responsibility for our families, schools, communities, corporations, religious organizations, states, and nation. The authors believe we must move beyond individual motivations to create institutions that nurture decisions based in the common good. They write: "Concerns that are most deeply personal are closely connected with concerns that are global in scope. We cannot be the caring people whom our children need us to be and ignore the world they will have to live in." This book, filled with common sense and moral wisdom, talks about "how to educate ourselves as citizens so that we really can 'make a difference' in the institutions that have such an impact on our lives."

Abstract: This book argues that, in spite of the complexities and difficulties, large-scale institutions are amenable to citizen action and the influence of global public opinion. Chapter 1 considers the problems Americans face today, why institutional dilemmas are also moral dilemmas, and why cultural resources are impoverished. Chapter 2 describes the historical forces that gave rise to the post-World War II society many Americans consider "normal." Subsequent developments continue to be measured by this postwar standard. Chapter 3 argues that the economy, an institutional arrangement created by humans, has profoundly influenced the kinds of people we have become. Chapter 4 considers the roles of government, law, and politics in developing a centralized state and examines the resulting loss of local control. Chapter 5 asks whether schools and universities can become democratic learning communities to help us deal with the moral and technical problems of a complex society. Chapter 6 considers the relationship between religious institutions and American society. Have they remained faithful to their defining messages, and do they help individuals and society meet current challenges? Chapter 7 describes the United States' changing role in the world system of powers, addressing the traditional ways we have thought about and acted in the world, how global pressures affect the kinds of people we are, and the growing necessity to increase our democratic learning capacity. The concluding chapter summarizes the issues of creativity and vitality in American institutional life, the importance of individual and social responsibility for institutions, and strategies for transforming the great society into the good society.

Berry, Wendell. *The Unsettling of America: Culture & Agriculture*. 3rd
    ed. San Francisco: Sierra Club Books, 1996.

Berry wrote this series of essays twenty years ago as a review of modern agriculture and agricultural policies. The work remains terrifically topical. He writes not simply of agriculture but about farming as a cultural development and spiritual discipline. He disagrees with the common assertion that all bad things, such as pollution, land destruction, and social upheaval, are inevitable. He advises how people all over the country can combat these evils by changing current policies and practices relating to the use of land: "To suggest that the health of places and communities might be the indispensable standard of economic behavior is finally to ask how a mere human, whose years are like the grass that is cut down in the evening, can justify on his or her own behalf the permanent destruction of anything."

Abstract: This book argues that agribusiness has been destructive not only to the lives of farmers but to society as a whole. Berry looks at misguided assumptions about industrial agriculture that have caused estrangement from the land, loss of community, devaluation of human work, and destruction of nature. The roots of these attitudes can be traced to the industrial revolution, which promised freedom from physical toil, and to the settlement of North America, which treated land, resources, and people as expendable. This history produces a disturbing (and officially sanctioned) vision of the farm of the future. For the sake of maximum production, technology will control the environment and men and women will have no place. Berry uses Henry County, Kentucky, where he grew up, as an example of the agricultural crisis and subsequent decline in culture. Since World War II, farms in Henry County have become increasingly mechanized, resulting in more abandoned land than ever before. The focus of interest has shifted largely from the household to the automobile, while the ideals of workmanship and thrift have been replaced by leisure, comfort, and entertainment. Young people expect to leave as soon as they finish high school because staying on the farm costs too much, requires too much work, and is hardly a fashionable ambition. Berry challenges cultivation techniques that damage the soil and sacrifice quality for quantity. He questions our reliance on the vast energy resources needed to fuel machines and manufacture chemicals. He denounces the "get big or get out" philosophy that has driven millions of farmers from the land and "unsettled" whole communities. Berry examines successful agricultural societies, such as the Amish, and contemporary marginal approaches, including homesteading, farm co-ops, alternative technologies, and peasant agriculture.

Vitek, William and Wes Jackson, eds. *Rooted in the Land: Essays on Community and Place.* New Haven: Yale University Press, 1996.

We state in the preface that our view of education has been influenced by individuals from an array of disciplines. In *Rooted in the Land*, philosophers, scientists, activists, economists, historians, farmers and ranchers, sociologists, theologians, and political scientists offer social and ecological perspectives on the nature of community. The authors add a new richness to our understanding of community and place. It gives us hope that authors from diverse backgrounds have converged around the importance of community and place. This diversity gives strength to the ideas and is necessary for changing our definition of living well.

Abstract: Many of these 31 essays comment on the role of education in promoting the transient, materialistic lifestyle. Others suggest ways education can foster place attachment and community development. Essays focused specifically on education discuss the rootlessness of college faculty, enlargement of social capital as newcomers "become native" to a place, need for a rural education of general knowledge and skills, and need for a moral education that supports civic life. The essays are "Rediscovering the Landscape" (William Vitek); "Leave If You Can" (Harry W. Paige); "The Rootless Professors" (Eric Zencey); "Pseudocommunities" (David Ehrenfeld); "From Monoculture to Polyculture" (Paul Custodio Bube); "An Amish Perspective" (David Kline); "The Common Life" (Scott Russell Sanders); "Living with the Land" (Helena Norberg-Hodge); "Defending Small Farms, Small Towns, and Good Work" (Lynn R. Miller); "Addicted to Work" (Linda M. Hasselstrom); "Conserving Communities" (Wendell Berry); "Does Community Have a Value? A Reply" (Carl D. Esbjornson); "Matfield Green" (Wes Jackson); "Dwelling: Making Peace with Space and Place" (Deborah Tall); "Coming In to the Foodshed" (Jack Kloppenburg Jr., John Hendrickson, G. W. Stevenson); "'Placed' between Promise and Command" (Walter Brueggemann); "Other Selves" (John A. Livingston); "Aldo Leopold as Hunter and Communitarian" (Franklin A. Kalinowski); "Aldo Leopold and the Values of the Native" (Gregory Cooper); "Biological Explanations and Environmental Expectations" (Kristin Shrader-Frechette); "Barn Raising" (Daniel Kemmis); "Community and the Virtue of Necessity" (William Vitek); "Defining Normative Community" (John B. Cobb Jr.); "In Search of Community" (Philip Selznick); "Redeeming the Land" (Richard Cartwright Austin); "Creating Social Capital" (Cornelia Butler Flora, Jan L. Flora); "Re-Ruralizing Education" (David W. Orr); "A Public Philosophy for Civic Culture" (William M. Sullivan); "Land: Challenge and Opportunity" (Susan Witt, Robert Swann); "Community-Supported Agriculture: Rediscovering Community" (Jack Kittredge); and "Community Farming in Massachusetts" (Brian Donahue).

Leopold, Aldo. *A Sand County Almanac and Sketches Here and There: With Other Essays on Conservation from Round River.* 2nd ed. New York: Oxford University Press, 1993.

Leopold described himself this way: "There are some who can live without wild things, and some who cannot. These essays are the delights and dilemmas of one who cannot." The father of wildlife conservation in America, Leopold is a warm, encouraging, amiable teacher. He uses his family's weekend experiences on a washed-out sand farm on the Wisconsin River to show readers the impact we have on the land. His elegant, accessible, poetic language seduces us into believing that a deep understanding of where we live "not only makes the world a more interesting place, but can give us direction and a basis for ethical human behavior." He humorously links the humanities and science to help us confront the value of wilderness, the costs of evaluating conservation exclusively in economic terms, and the development of an ethic based on ecology.

Abstract: Part I of this book traces the monthly changes in the Wisconsin countryside for a whole year. Part II consists of essays Leopold wrote over a 40-year period as he traveled around the woodlands of Wisconsin, Iowa, Arizona, Sonora, Oregon, and Manitoba. Leopold invokes a theme of environmental loss with accounts of crane marshes being drained, wild rivers being dammed, bears and wolves being extirpated, and invasive alien grasses taking over native prairies. In the last section, Leopold addresses the philosophical issues involved in wildlife conservation, including the nature of "sportsmanship" in America and the ethical call to love and respect the land. These essays address the political, cultural, social, and educational issues needed to change our fundamental relationship with the land.

McPhee, John. *The Second John McPhee Reader.* Compiled by David Remnick and Patricia Strachan. New York: Noonday Press, 1996.

Thrills! Chills! Spills! The Earth Moves! This is the ultimate back-to-basics primer. McPhee's best-selling account of the earth's formation makes geology gripping, funny, and deeply engrossing. This is nonfiction at its best. Difficult subjects become clear and fascinating to readers. McPhee finds craftsmen who care deeply about their work and draws stories from scientists that open up new worlds to the rest of us. He gives us new eyes, new ears, and a new appreciation for our earthly home. You will never walk outside the same way after reading this book, and you can amaze your friends with tidbits such as, "Did you know that Nevada and New Jersey are very similar tectonically?"

Abstract: This volume includes excerpts from the author's 11 nonfiction books published since 1975: *Coming Into the Country* (1977) describes Alaska and its people; *Giving Good Weight: A Collection* (1979) relates McPhee's experience selling produce in New York City's Greenmarket Program and profiles a Spanish chef who returned to Europe after years of cooking in rural Pennsylvania; *Basin and Range* (1981) recounts McPhee's travels with geologists while charting North American continental shifts; *In Suspect Terrain* (1983) tells the story of Anita Harris, a scientist with the United States Geological Survey, who explored the Appalachian region and its people; *La Place De La Concorde Suisse* (1984) details McPhee's experiences on patrol with a battalion of the Swiss Army; *Table of Contents* (1985) discusses a flying game warden in northern Maine also named John McPhee, bear cubs in Pennsylvania, and young doctors in rural Maine; *Rising From the Plains* (1986) includes the life experiences of a one-room-school teacher in Wyoming during the early nineteenth century; *The Control of Nature* (1989) depicts three situations in which human beings, impelled by economic forces, are engaged in battles with nature, including flowing lava in Iceland, debris from disintegrating mountains in Los Angeles, and flooding on the Mississippi River; *Looking For a Ship* (1990) describes the author's journey on a U.S. merchant marine ship to the west coast of South America; *Assembling California* (1993) details McPhee's travels with tectonophysicist Eldridge Moores and illustrates how human and geologic time intersect, as evidenced by the California gold rush of 1849 and the Loma Prieta earthquake of 1989; and *The Ransom of Russian Art* (1994) relates the story of Norton T. Dodge, an American professor who smuggled nonconformist artworks from the Soviet Union between the 1950s and 1970s.

A Sense of Civic Involvement:
Education for Living Well Politically

Parsons, Cynthia. *Serving to Learn, Learning to Serve: Civics and Service from A to Z.* Thousand Oaks, CA: Corwin Press, 1995.

This small book is a fine compilation of service-learning theory and experiences for young people with an emphasis on civic involvement. Written by the former education editor of the *Christian Science Monitor*, the text is clear, firm, and insightful. In one example, Parsons tells the story of a high school principal who sent congratulatory letters to each of her students on their eighteenth birthday, welcoming them to the fellowship of voters.

Abstract: This book espouses service learning as an important and integral part of school for students. The 26 short chapters are based on the letters of the alphabet: awards and appreciation; books and birthdays; civics, civility, and concern; daring and doing; equity; French and other foreign languages; government; helping; interns; justice; kindness; "Like What?" and liability; money; natural science; obligation; physical education; quid pro quo; recreation; SerVermont; time and transportation; United States; value; who; xenophilia; youth; and zeal.

Sandel, Michael J. *Democracy's Discontent: America in Search of a Public Philosophy.* Cambridge: Belknap Press of Harvard University Press, 1996.

Thomas Jefferson insisted that giving information to the people was the most certain engine of democracy: "Educate and inform the whole mass of people. Enable them to see that it is in their interest to preserve peace and order, and they will preserve them. . . . They are the only sure reliance for the preservation of our liberty." This fundamental purpose of education has been marginalized, made invisible by talk of preparation for the global economy and self-aggrandizement above all. As a result, rural people have been denied the education that equips them to advocate for themselves and their place. Rural education, based on an industrial model, has been just another extractive industry, capturing local taxes while young people leave the community. Teaching ourselves to participate in this democracy requires a new public philosophy, one that reinvigorates civic life. Sandel's book is a fine primer on where we are, how we got there, and where we might go together.

Abstract: This book suggests American politics is rife with discontent despite unprecedented affluence, greater social justice for women and minorities, and the end of the Cold War. Sandel believes liberalism has allowed the government to assume a position of neutrality with respect to the moral choices and values of its citizens. By treating actions not as right or wrong but merely as "harmful" or "not harmful" to society, liberal politics has become disconnected from the real experience of most Americans. In essence, American politics has lost its civic voice, leaving both liberals and conservatives unable to inspire the sense of community and civic engagement that self-government requires. Sandel searches the American political experience for a public philosophy adequate to our time. He recalls the arguments of Thomas Jefferson and Alexander Hamilton, Abraham Lincoln and Stephen Douglas, Oliver Wendell Holmes and Louis Brandeis, and Franklin Roosevelt and Ronald Reagan. He relates everything from debates over slavery and industrial capitalism to contemporary controversies over the welfare state, religion, abortion, gay rights, and hate speech. The book also addresses rights and the neutral state; religious liberty and freedom of speech; privacy rights and family law; economics and virtue in the early republic; free labor versus wage labor; community, self-government, and progressive reform; liberalism and the Keynesian Revolution; and the triumph and travail of the procedural republic. Sandel calls for a revitalization of America's civic republican tradition that would shift politics from a political economy of growth to a political economy of citizenship and self-government.

Davidson, Osha Gray. *Broken Heartland: The Rise of America's Rural Ghetto*. New York: Free Press, 1990; Iowa City: University of Iowa Press, 1996.

A reporter who spent three years in Mechanicsville, Iowa, Davidson has written a wonderful case study of a small rural town that could be Anywhere, USA. *Broken Heartland* moves the farm crisis from sterile headlines to the real lives of people about whom the reader comes to care deeply. This book is used in a number of high school classes as a jumping-off place for local research. Students typically react, "This is real and it's about us." A fine example of investigative journalism, the book is a page-turner even when dealing with the intricacies of agricultural policy. The expanded 1996 version revisits the research, most of which was done between 1986 and 1989.

Abstract: This book addresses the disintegration of rural communities and the spread of homelessness, hunger, poverty, and despair throughout the nation's Heartland. It is based on interviews with more than 200 residents, social workers, government officials, and scholars in rural Iowa communities. An examination of the farm crisis is necessary in order to understand the decline of America's Heartland. Total farm debt climbed from about $50 billion in 1971 to over $200 billion in 1986. Foreign markets dried up, interest rates jumped, land values plummeted, government funds were reduced, and the thin mantle on which farmers had built their operations gave way. The resulting devastation was quickly dubbed the "farm crisis." However, it was really a rural community crisis, because it impacted every facet of rural life. The result has been the transformation of healthy, mostly middle-class communities into rural ghettos—pockets of poverty, unemployment, violence, and despair. The dimensions of the problem are sobering: between 54 and 60 million rural Americans, one-quarter of the country's population, are touched by the decline. In Iowa, the hardest hit of all Midwestern states, one of six individuals falls below the federal poverty line, and, in some counties, the poverty rate approaches thirty percent. Davidson contends that recent trends in rural economic development, such as industrial recruitment, free-enterprise zone designations, and the proliferation of home workers, have actually deepened rural problems. To attack the problems of rural ghettos, we must first confront agricultural problems, because farming remains the cornerstone of small-town life and the rural economy. Reforming agricultural policy so that efficient, family-sized farms are given a chance to prosper is only a starting point in crafting a strategy for rural development. In the final analysis, what rural America needs most is not more jobs or money, but more democracy—in the form of citizenry willing and able to participate fully in the development and sustenance of their communities.

Mathews, David. *Is There a Public for Public Schools?* Dayton, OH: Kettering Foundation Press, 1996, 1997.

Reporting on the results of more than a decade of research by the Kettering Foundation, Mathews looks closely at the relationship between the public and public education. What does the public consider quality education? What are the perceptions of public education as it exists today? He asks, "Is there any correlation between the public life of a community and the quality of its public schools?" The research supports a strong correlation between healthy public life and quality public education. Mathews offers strategies for building a sense of community and working together for quality public education.

Abstract: Despite a long tradition of support for public education, America's commitment to public schools is eroding. This book tells why. Presenting the view that schools are extensions of their communities, Mathews argues community development must precede educational reform. Fundamental change must start within the community to overcome structural impediments and improve school systems. The final chapter describes how to make public life vigorous and healthy and introduces a new paradigm for understanding communities.

Barber, Benjamin R. *An Aristocracy of Everyone: The Politics of Education and the Future of America.* New York: Ballantine Books, 1992; New York: Oxford University Press, 1994.

This work revives the idea of citizenship and democracy as a way of life rather than just a political system. Barber quotes Woodrow Wilson: "As a nation we are becoming civically illiterate. Unless we find better ways to educate ourselves as citizens, we run the risk of drifting unwittingly into a new kind of Dark Age—a time when small cadres of specialists will control knowledge and thus control the decision-making process." Barber rejects the notion of a so-called canon of accepted history and literary texts. He demonstrates that our national story comprises an intermingling of diverse, contradictory, and often subversive voices. Here you will learn about teaching democracy through community service. While many of Barber's examples are from postsecondary education, teachers at every level will find this information provocative and useful.

Abstract: This book argues that rather than debating who should be taught, what should be taught, and how it should be paid for, Americans should address education as the wellspring of democracy. By emphasizing democracy as much as the pursuit of excellence, young Americans will gain an apprenticeship in liberty, grounded in a renewed commitment to community service. This approach provides Americans with the literacy to live in a civil society and the competence to participate in democratic communities. At the same time, it promotes an excellence in education to maintain America's economic, technical, and political preeminence in a rapidly changing world. Education offers the only path toward rebuilding and reinvigorating the United States; this is a path that must be followed now.

A Sense of Worth:
Education for Living Well Economically

Kemmis, Daniel. *Community and the Politics of Place.* Norman: University of Oklahoma Press, 1990, 1992.

This is the best civics lesson one can buy. In one hundred fifty pages, Kemmis takes us back to Shay's Rebellion and shows that the consequent debates between Jefferson and Hamilton helped produce the dysfunctional political process we experience today. He argues persuasively that our politics of "keeping citizens apart" prevents civic action for the public good. He draws on his experiences in Montana, as a member of the state house of representatives and mayor of Missoula, to demonstrate how the political process can work differently. In the last chapter, Kemmis expresses the necessity of *inhabiting* one's place and describes the politics of re-inhabitation. This book should be kept handy and re-read whenever political cynicism becomes too great.

Abstract: The preamble to Montana's constitution expresses gratitude for Montana's landscape and reflects that the political culture of a place is tied to the place itself. By the same token, political culture must be strengthened in the context of very specific places by people struggling to live well in such places. This book examines how a revival of public life and civic culture could happen, focusing on the West, Montana, and Missoula. Kemmis explores how Jefferson's notion of an educated citizenry acting for the common good was overcome by the federalist procedural republic, involving special interest groups and a system of checks and balances. Kemmis examines public education for citizenship in the context of the American political empire and the closing of the frontier. He contrasts current Montana politics, in which discussions and projects are stalemated by territoriality and alienation, with earlier times when the need to help neighbors in a rugged environment promoted community cooperation and tolerance.

Steinbeck, John. *The Grapes of Wrath.* New York: The Viking Press, 1939; New York: Penguin USA, 1992.

This classic novel tells the story of the three-generation Joad family of Oklahoma and their migration to California. Steinbeck brings a human scale to the devastating results of the 1930s' farm policies, Depression, and drought. The Joads are not strangers or outsiders, but people we come to care about through wonderful storytelling. Steinbeck intended to shock people into thinking about economic inequities in America, not to write specifically about rural issues. This prizewinning novel does both and creates a natural bridge between literature and the lives of rural students.

Smiley, Jane. *A Thousand Acres.* New York: Knopf, 1991; New York: Ivy Books, 1996.

Lest anyone thinks the Joads are history, Smiley brings her remarkable storytelling talents to the current farm crisis. An Iowa family experiences the effects of the "get big or get out" paradigm on individuals, towns, and local culture. Smiley writes lyrically about the pleasures of living in the country, such as drinking a cup of coffee on the porch in the quiet of the early morning, bonding with the land, and belonging to the community. She also writes powerfully of the pain involved when these things come apart. As topical as this morning's headlines, this novel inspires thoughtful reflection about what it means to be rural in contemporary America.

Bingham, Sam. *The Last Ranch: A Colorado Community and the Coming Desert.* New York: Pantheon Books, 1996; San Diego: Harcourt Brace, 1997.

The Last Ranch tells the true story of the Whitten family's struggle to prevent their land from becoming a desert. Bingham brings a journalist's clear eye and an outsider's objectivity to conflicts over grazing rights and the private use of public land. He paints a complex interplay between human society and the natural world as stark as the faces of the ranchers and the hardpan of the land. These are hard lives in hard times. The transformations of one community, the American West, and the land itself are illuminated in this powerful book. The author ends his story: "People who must act *must* hope. People who hope must act, not always correctly but always creatively, and they will not let the world end in desert."

Abstract: The San Luis Valley is a broad, expansive range ringed by massive mountains that has only about eight inches of rain a year. The soil is coarse, sandy, and hostile to cultivation. Ranched heavily since the 1840s, the land is all but denuded of native vegetation. In addition, artesian wells that once shot water twenty feet in the air now require pumping. It is also a place where a small enclave of ranchers struggles to make a living, fighting not only the elements but a host of other forces including politics, the pressures of modern culture and technology, and the marketplace. The book focuses on the story of Donnie and Karen Whitten, high school sweethearts who live in a double-wide trailer on a ranch with their three children. The Whittens and their neighbors attempt to forge a new path in the management of their land, finding alternative and often radical measures to stop the coming desert. The Whittens are influenced by a number of

interesting characters: a holistic, ranch-management expert, whose perceptions were honed in an African civil war; a mathematical genius who wins
a legal case for the ranchers despite overwhelming odds; and Bud Williams,
who can move a herd of cattle into a corral simply by putting his hands in
his pockets and walking toward them. Bingham concludes that the condition of the San Luis Valley is scarcely different from that of drought-
stricken Africa. He suggests famine in the African drylands makes news
while American famine does not because the media covers agricultural
issues poorly.

Hanson, Victor Davis. *Fields Without Dreams: Defending the Agrarian*
Idea. New York: Free Press, 1996, 1997.

A fifth-generation California vine and fruit grower (and Greek scholar),
Hanson writes about the real connections between family farms and the
virtues and work ethic that undergird our society. America has given up on
a concept that goes back to the Greek *polis*: families who inherit land and
grow food are rewarded with lives in which their children are fed and
clothed. *Such agrarianism had value to all beyond the confines of the farm*
(emphasis added by authors). Here is a different take on what it means to
live in community.

Abstract: This book chronicles the decline of the American family
farm and the rise of modern agribusiness. Hanson suggests the loss of
agrarianism is at the root of many of the ills that plague modern society—
materialism, crime, and spiritual emptiness. He predicts the federal system
of large-scale, agricultural subsidies will destroy farmers' way of life.
Hanson also relates how his family faced an overwhelming personal crisis
when the great "raisin boom" of the 1970s was followed by the great "raisin
crash" of the 1980s. In 1983, a glut of foreign raisins coupled with domestic
overproduction caused the price of raisins to plummet from $1,300 to $450
a ton, devastating farmers in the San Joaquin Valley. To save their farm,
Hanson's family increased their debt to farm another piece of land and, for
the first time in 117 years, they rented out property to compensate for their
vanishing capital. The title of the book, *Fields Without Dreams*, represents
an agrarian Armageddon where the family farm, both as a way of life and a
reassuring image of the mind, is being obliterated.

Fisher, Stephen L., ed. *Fighting Back in Appalachia: Traditions of*
Resistance and Change. Philadelphia: Temple University Press, 1992,
1993.

These 16 essays relate research on change-oriented movements in Appalachia since 1960 to broader discussions within academic and community-
organizing circles. Through personal narratives and formal analysis, they

document how particular resistance efforts arose and why they succeeded or failed. How have issues of race, class, gender, and culture shaped resistance efforts? What impact have global and national structures and events had on local movements for change? What is legitimate about the notion of regional identity? And finally, what organizing strategies make sense for the future? All people interested in organizing movements to change rural America will find these examples insightful.

Abstract: This book places Appalachian community resistance and struggle in the context of dissent nationally. Of particular educational relevance are chapters describing the Highlander Research and Education Center in eastern Tennessee which encourages activist networks and the creation of a social movement in Appalachia; organizations that provide job training for women seeking to enter traditional male occupations; cultural education and the rebirth of culture as forces in regional identity and community organizing; and the political implications of Appalachian studies and related postmodernist thought. Chapters are "Stopping the Bulldozers: What Difference Did It Make?" (M. B. Bingman); "Like a Flower Slowly Blooming: Highlander and the Nurturing of an Appalachian Movement" (J. M. Glen); "Racism and Organizing in Appalachia" (D. Manning-Miller); "From Fussin' to Organizing: Individual and Collective Resistance at Yellow Creek" (S. Cable); "Save Our Cumberland Mountains: Growth and Change within a Grassroots Organization" (B. Allen); "Practical Lessons in Community Organizing in Appalachia: What We've Learned at Kentuckians for the Commonwealth" (J. Szakos); "The Community Farm Alliance in Kentucky: The Growth, Mistakes, and Lessons of the Farm Movement of the 1980s" (H. Hamilton & E. Ryan); "Appalachian Women Fight Back: Organizational Approaches to Nontraditional Job Advocacy" (C. Weiss); "The Memory of Miners and the Conscience of Capital: Coal Miners' Strikes as Free Spaces" (R. A. Couto); "Singing across Dark Spaces: The Union/Community Takeover of Pittston's Moss 3 Plant" (J. Sessions & F. Ansley);" The People's Respirator: Coalition Building and the Black Lung Association" (B. M. Judkins); "Sowing on the Mountain: Nurturing Cultural Roots and Creativity for Community Change" (G. Carawan & C. Carawan); "Engendering the Struggle: Women's Labor and Traditions of Resistance in Rural Southern Appalachia" (M. K. Anglin); "Appalachian Studies, Resistance, and Postmodernism" (A. Banks, D. Billings, & K. Tice); "Politics, Expressive Form, and Historical Knowledge in a Blue Ridge Resistance Movement" (S. W. Foster); and "Conclusion: New Populist Theory and the Study of Dissent in Appalachia" (S. L. Fisher).

Stull, Donald D., Michael J. Broadway, and David Griffith, eds. *Any Way You Cut It: Meat Processing and Small-Town America (Rural America).* Lawrence: University Press of Kansas, 1995.

Processing plants for meat, poultry, and fish comprise the single largest growth industry in rural America. Stull and his associates have written a muckraking book about the packing industry. They look at how the industry imports and abandons individuals, many of whom are minorities. Importantly, they also stress the impact on communities where these plants are located, pointing out the social costs of this form of economic development.

Abstract: The introductory essay, "Making Meat," by David Griffith, Michael J. Broadway, and Donald D. Stull, examines the impact of the food-processing industry on rural development, including policy and theoretical implications. This article summarizes related themes from other essays, including the routine victimization of workers and communities; high injury rates; government's role in extending public subsidies to these firms through tax incentives and exemptions, job training and commodity programs; the growing importance of immigrant workers; and the impact on immigration policy, trade negotiations, and economic restructuring. Other essays include "From City to Countryside: Recent Changes in the Structure and Location of the Meat- and Fish-Processing Industries" (Michael Broadway); "On the Horns of a Dilemma: The U.S. Meat and Poultry Industry" (Steve Bjerklie); "Killing Them Softly: Work in Meatpacking Plants and What It Does to Workers" (Donald D. Stull and Michael J. Broadway); "Dances with Cows: Beefpacking's Impact on Garden City, Kansas, and Lexington, Nebraska" (Lourdes Gouveia and Donald D. Stull); "Pork, Poultry, and Newcomers in Storm Lake, Iowa" (Mark A. Grey); "Hay Trabajo: Poultry Processing, Rural Industrialization, and the Latinization of Low-Wage Labor" (David Griffith); "New Immigrants in an Old Industry: Blue Crab Processing in Pamlico County, North Carolina" (David Griffith); "Industries, Immigrants, and Illness in the New Midwest" (Robert A. Hackenberg and Gary Kukulka); "The Kill Line: Facts of Life, Proposals for Change" (Bob Hall); and "Joe Hill Died for Your Sins: Empowering Minority Workers in the New Industrial Labor Force" (Robert A. Hackenberg).

A Sense of Connection:
Education for Living Well Spiritually

Cajete, Gregory. *Look to the Mountain: An Ecology of Indigenous Education.* Durango, CO: Kivaki Press, 1994.

Cajete, an American Indian educator, has created an educational theory of context. Rather than pitting one set of cultural values against another, he shows that, to be effective, any proposition or doctrine must find a comfortable home in its specific community. Cajete brings to bear the traditions and insights of a number of tribal cultures as he helps us find new, creative, and sophisticated approaches to bridge the differences between Indian and non-Indian education.

Abstract: This book explores the nature of indigenous education, outlining key elements of American Indian perspectives on learning and teaching. Cajete advocates a contemporary, culturally based educational process founded upon traditional tribal values, orientations, and principles while simultaneously using modern education's most appropriate concepts, technologies, and content. Environmental relationship, myth, visionary traditions, traditional arts, tribal community, and nature-centered spirituality are the essences of American Indian life for discovering one's true face (character, potential, identity), heart (soul, creative self, true passion), and foundation (true work, vocation), all of which lead to the expression of a complete life. Indigenous education, grounded in the basics of human nature, provides new ways of teaching ecological thinking and environmental sustainability. It has the potential not only to transform what is misnamed "Indian education" but to transform modern American education. Cajete discusses seven core courses for an indigenous science curriculum in relation to the seven cardinal directions honored by all indigenous peoples.

Kawagley, A. Oscar. *A Yupiaq Worldview: A Pathway to Ecology and Spirit.* Prospect Heights, IL: Waveland Press, 1995.

Kawagley proposes a teaching method that incorporates Western science and his own Yupiaq culture. He intersperses memories of his Yupiaq grandmother, who taught him to respect the reciprocity of nature, with the science he learned in Western schools. Kawagley contrasts the traditional ways of the world with the lives faced by Yupiaq people today. This constellation of values and life principles brings together indigenous and Western views to create a new school curriculum. He envisions "taking the best from the two worlds and reconstructing a world to fit the times."

Abstract: Chapter 1 discusses the worldviews of Alaska Natives (specifically the Yupiaq), which is based on maintaining a balance among the human, natural, and spiritual worlds. The Yupiaq believe in the equality of all creatures, learning through participant observation, sharing, coopera-tion, respect for the wisdom of elders, and an intimate knowledge of the local landscape. Chapter 2 provides a brief history of the Yupiit Nation and its school system and describes the research site of Akiak on the Kuskokwim River in southwestern Alaska. Chapter 3 examines Yupiaq use of science, mathematics, and technology for survival. Subjects include weather predic-tion, fishing, fish preparation and preservation, diet and nutrition, tradi-tional medicines and admonitions, healing and mental health, and integra-tion of modern technology. Chapter 4 describes educational practices and science instruction in Akiak's K-12 school. Chapter 5 discusses Yupiaq cultural adaptation in the contemporary world, the cultural "price" of introducing outside technologies, the implications of Yupiaq ethnoscience for village schooling, and the need to integrate schooling and Yupiaq ways of knowing. Goals are proposed for culturally integrated schooling, and a science curriculum is outlined based on the Yupiaq fish camp experience.

Jackson, Wes. *Altars of Unhewn Stone: Science and the Earth.* San Francisco: North Point Press, 1987.

This series of essays takes you into the mind of Wes Jackson of the Land Institute. "Eleven originated out of irritation, three out of joy, and four for my own clarification. . . . I don't apologize for the imbalance between irritation and joy. We all live in a world of wounds." He writes from the perspective of an evolutionary biologist turned civic activist. His integra-tion of hard science and spirituality is remarkable: "We sustain our focus by constantly measuring our work against the standards set by nature's prairie. But we also freely explore the social, political, economic, and religious implications of the way humans have to live and work the land that sustains us." His voice is strong, confrontational, and leavened with great love for his fellow, fallible human beings.

Abstract: The title of this book was taken from Exodus 20:25 which instructs Moses to build an altar of unhewn stone "for if thou lift up thy tool upon it, thou hast polluted it." The book calls for agricultural practices that will not destroy human or biological communities, that will minimize soil erosion and reliance on chemicals and fossil fuels, and that will preserve the information contained in the genetic codes of plants and animals threatened with extinction. Other topics include the danger of valuing scientific and technical information over cultural information, the empty promises and high costs of biotechnology, the basic requirements for building a sustain-able society and becoming stewards of the land, how economics and colonization have destroyed Native cultures and rural communities, the sources of farm debt, and the falsehoods of farming. Jackson proposes that the development of sustainable agriculture requires wisdom about traditional farming attitudes and the use of land and resources. Consideration must also be given to the interrelations of cultural and biological communities.

Grahame, Kenneth. *The Wind in the Willows.* New York: Scribner, 1960; New York: St. Martin's Press, 1996.

A fable of animals living together in rural England, this classic children's book has a strong sense of nature as a presence, particularly in the chapter titled "Piper at the Gates of Dawn." It is a wonderful read for people of every age and could not be farther in tone from the Disney movie of the same title.

Wood, Douglas. *Old Turtle.* Duluth, MN: Pfeifer-Hamilton Publishers, 1992.

The fable of *Old Turtle* begins, "Once, long long ago . . . yet somehow, not so very long . . . when all the beings of the world could speak . . . and understand one another. . . ." An argument begins when Old Turtle, who "hardly ever said anything," speaks of what is and what will become. With wisdom, in a time too busy to be still, Old Turtle asks all the beings of the world to "STOP. . . . And to see God in one another . . . and in the beauty of all the Earth." Through the story of Old Turtle, Wood tells lyrically of the power of all creation and the power of the One who creates. The quiet magic of *Old Turtle* asks us to listen, hear, and see what is beautiful in the earth and in each other.

Baylor, Byrd. *I'm in Charge of Celebrations.* New York: Scribner, 1986; New York: Aladdin Paperbacks, 1995.

Rainbow Celebration Day, Green Cloud Day, Coyote Day, and the Time of the Falling Stars are a few of the many events chosen by the one in charge of celebrations, a young American Indian girl living in the Southwest. When you are in charge of celebrations, you are never lonely. Baylor looks for special celebrations in the Southwest desert and finds them all around her. She celebrates "with horned toads and ravens and lizards and quail. . . . And, Friend, it's not a bad party." Baylor's book will make you, too, want to keep a notebook of the celebrations around you—the times "when your heart will POUND and you'll feel like you're standing on top of a mountain and you'll catch your breath like you were breathing some new kind of air."

Lopez, Barry. *The Rediscovery of North America.* Lexington: University Press of Kentucky, 1991; New York: Vintage Books, 1992.

In *The Rediscovery of North America,* Lopez challenges us "to see the land with a less acquisitive frame of mind." He believes we need to make the land our home and be responsible to that home. Lopez shines a bright light on the incursion of Christopher Columbus and today's continued destruction of our land and waters. He encourages us to "come to know the land, to discover what more may be there than merchantable timber, grazeable prairies, recoverable ores, damable water, netable fish . . .[to look] upon the land not as its possessor but as a companion." *The Rediscovery of North America* calls us to make a home within this land we inhabit.

Abstract: This book reexamines the underlying imperial attitudes of the European settlement of America beginning with the Spanish conquest. It is not known what Columbus and his men envisioned when they came ashore on San Salvador in 1492. But, in the name of distant and abstract powers, the Spanish seized the land and terrorized the people with murder, rape, theft, kidnaping, vandalism, child molestation, and acts of cruelty and humiliation. Europeans considered this conquest an imperial right, conferred by God, sanctioned by the state, and enforced by militia. This assumption of superiority over resident people was based not on morality but on race and cultural comparisons. This theme reverberates in the journals of people on the Oregon Trail, in the public speeches of nineteenth-century industrialists, and in twentieth-century politics; therefore, what Columbus began is not isolated in the past. Another victim of this demand for material wealth has been the land on which we live, evidenced by the acid-burned forests of New Hampshire, the cauterized soils of Iowa, and the collapse of the San Joaquin Valley into caverns emptied of their fossil waters. We have lost whole communities of people, plants, and animals, because a handful of men wanted gold and silver, title to land, and the privileges of aristocracy. We have sacrificed languages, epistemologies, books, ceremonies, systems of logic, and metaphysics. The trouble with the New World is that, from the beginning, we have imposed, not proposed. We said what we thought and bent to our will whatever resisted. The true wealth America offers—wealth that can turn exploitation into stewardship and greed into harmony—comes from the cultivation of local knowledge. Lopez "rediscovers" the New World not as a source of personal wealth but as a home, a place from which to draw strength and character.

Lopez, Barry. *Crow and Weasel.* San Francisco: North Point Press, 1990; New York: HarperPerennial, 1993.

Near the end of this fable, Weasel says, "Sometimes it is what is beautiful that carries you." Indeed, it is what is beautiful that carries young

Crow and Weasel from their homes and families in the South further north
than any of their people had ever traveled. They are carried by the beauties
of friendship, trust, tradition, respect, skill, and tolerance. On their journey,
they see things never seen before: deep forests of tall pine, large-footed
caribou, and the flat-faced Inuit people who travel in boats of many skins.
Crow and Weasel meet new friends—Mouse, Badger, and Grizzly—who
share their talents with them and provide safety, shelter, food, and kindness.
Crow and Weasel respond by offering friendship, gifts, and respect. They
return to their people in the South wiser and stronger. Crow and Weasel are
entrusted to keep and share the tales of their journey: "The stories people
tell have a way of taking care of them. If stories come to you, care for them.
And learn to give them away where they are needed. Sometimes a person
needs a story more than food to stay alive. That is why we put these stories
in each other's memory. This is how people care for themselves." Lopez
beautifully tells the story of *Crow and Weasel*, teaching others how to care
for themselves. We are reminded: "It is good to be alive. To have friends, to
have a family, to have children, to live in a particular place. These relationships are sacred."

Hasselstrom, Linda M. *Land Circle: Writings Collected from the Land.*
Golden, CO: Fulcrum Publishing, 1991, 1993.

Hasselstrom is the type of person David Orr describes as a "homecomer."
She grew up on a ranch in western South Dakota, left as a young adult, and
returned to find her life as a rancher and writer. *Land Circle* is a series of
essays and poems about coming home and living as a very modern woman
in the West. In down-to-earth language, she describes the deeply spiritual
connections she finds with the land, her neighbors, and her work. Her
language sings with the power of the prairie wind. Here is a strong woman,
struggling with what it means to come home.

Abstract: Hasselstrom explores her connection with the land and the
circle of life. An introductory essay addresses the economic status of the
Great Plains and the resulting impact on environmental issues. The book is
divided into three sections, subtitled "Where Neighbor is a Verb"; "George:
In Beauty Walk"; and "A Woman's Covenant." Hasselstrom relates the
culture and values associated with living on the ranch. She writes about
feeding her cattle when the temperature is 30 degrees below zero, deliver-
ing newborn calves, slaughtering cows for food, watching a wildfire come
dangerously close to her pastures, and experiencing joy and satisfaction
through her love of the land. Other essays address the cycle of birth and
death; her love for her husband and how she came to terms with his
untimely illness and death; her attempts as a part-time writing instructor to
teach college students an appreciation and respect for the environment; the

value of protecting both national parks and private lands; the rights of cattle ranchers versus animal-rights activists; the reason she carries a gun; and the close relationship she has with her stepchildren.

Kingsolver, Barbara. *High Tide in Tucson: Essays from Now or Never.* New York: HarperCollins, 1995; New York: HarperPerennial, 1996.

Fans of Barbara Kingsolver's fiction need no encouragement to read her thoughts on life or anything else. New readers can anticipate the joy of meeting a fascinating friend. This collection of essays begins with the story of Buster, a hermit crab that stowed away in the Bahamas, came home to Tucson in her shorts pocket, and continues to move to the rhythms of the tides. She shares her thoughts about how we are connected: "What a stroke of luck. What a singular brute feat of outrageous fortune: to be born to citizenship in the Animal Kingdom. We love and we lose, go back to the start and do it right over again. For every heavy forebrain solemnly cataloging the facts of a harsh landscape, there's a rush of intuition behind it crying out: High tide!" Essays on family, place, growing up in rural Kentucky, the miracle of libraries and caring librarians, and community relations will send you out rejoicing as well.

Abstract: This collection of 25 essays covers such topics as survival instincts in the face of relocation or personal upheaval; coming to terms with the desert environment around a new home; reminiscences of not fitting into high school social life in small-town Kentucky; how a librarian saved an alienated teenager by introducing her to the mysteries and joys of the library; fashion versus style; the evolution of housework; fidelity across species; discipline and two-year olds; balancing motherhood and a writing career; the current anti-child political agenda; travels in Hawaii, Benin, and the Canary Islands; valuing today's nontraditional families; erasing Native American stereotypes; whether a writer should depict other races and cultures; attachment to the place of one's childhood; the continuing threat of nuclear war; the writer's responsibility to tell unpleasant truths about national politics; the effects of mass-media violence; and fostering imagination and creativity. (SV)

Berry, Wendell. *The Gift of Good Land: Further Essays, Cultural and Agricultural.* San Francisco: North Point Press, 1981, 1983.

This collection of wonderful essays includes 14 standards by which decisions and solutions can be judged. These stories about Berry's friends and neighbors illustrate the practical, economic, and moral aspects of such actions as growing crops, raising animals, and bringing up a family. He approaches life like an Old Testament prophet, accentuating the connections between spirituality and lives lived well: "To use knowledge and tools in a particular place with good long-term results is not heroic. . . . It is a small action, but more complex and difficult, more skillful and responsible, more whole and enduring, than most grand actions. It comes of a willingness to devote oneself to work that perhaps only the eye of Heaven will see in its full intricacy and excellence. Perhaps the real work, like real prayer and real charity, must be done in secret."

Abstract: Berry's essays stress the interdependence of nature, the problems related to agricultural practices, and the resulting loss of rural land, culture, and community. Berry reiterates that good agriculture is synonymous with small-scale agriculture, conventionally called the "small farm." Larger farms are more likely to specialize in one or two crops, have no animals, and depend on chemicals, purchased supplies, and credit. Berry proposes that the present system of industrial agriculture is failing because it is incapable of providing even rudimentary methods of soil conservation or the restraints necessary for the survival of rural neighborhoods. Berry journeyed to the Peruvian Andes, southern Arizona desert, and Amish country to study the evolution of ancient, native agricultural practices. In the title essay, he compares Judeo-Christian heritage with the Buddhist doctrine of "right livelihood" or "right occupation." Other essays deal with homesteading, tools, horses and tractors, family work, land reclamation, and diversity of land use. Berry argues compellingly that the "gift" of good land is on loan as long as the recipients practice responsible stewardship.

Rogers, Mary Beth. *Cold Anger: A Story of Faith and Power Politics.* Denton: University of North Texas Press, 1990.

Cold Anger is about a new kind of intervention in politics: poor working people who incorporate their religious values into a struggle for power and visibility. It is about women and men who promote public and private hope, political and personal responsibility, and community and individual transformation. From the prologue of this book, we are caught. Rogers tells the story of Ernesto Cortes and his colleagues at the Industrial Areas Foundation (IAF) as they invent new ways to organize middle-class and poor working people to share in the power that follows money. Teaching, nurturing, confronting, negotiating, compromising, giving, and receiving are all part of this organizing strategy. This philosophy is centered in relationships that come from working side-by-side with people. Relationships with adversaries are valued as well, leaving the door open for opponents to become allies in future causes.

Abstract: Almost unnoticed, growing numbers of poor working people are entering community politics in dozens of major cities in Texas and across the nation. They are unusual because they view politics as a long-term process to build relationships, new institutions, and humane communities. They are sparked by people like Ernesto Cortes, Jr., an extraordinary community organizer who is engaged in the empowerment of people at the neighborhood and parish level. Cortes and the IAF network of community organizations have become successful enough to transform the politics of San Antonio and influence the fate of statewide issues. Moreover, IAF groups are virtually the only organizations in the nation that entice poor working people to participate in politics. The chapters are anecdotal, covering episodes in Cortes's life; the history of the IAF; and San Antonio, Chicago, and Los Angeles politics from 1964 to 1990, primarily the 1980s. These stories demonstrate the role of local churches and personal faith in community organization and the struggle for social justice, the interpersonal strategies used in IAF training programs for church leaders and community activists, and the importance of "relational" power that grows out of the mutual accountability of members of local organizations.

Trimble, Stephen and Terry Tempest Williams, eds. *Testimony: Writers of the West Speak on Behalf of Utah Wilderness.* Minneapolis: Milkweed Editions, 1996.

Bill Bradley, while serving in the U.S. Senate, called this collection "an act of public service." It represents a new form of political action. Twenty-one prominent writers submitted these essays and poems to Congress, communicating the urgent need to preserve threatened lands. This work influenced the debate and final vote on the establishment of the Utah Public Lands Management Act. The book lists United States Wilderness Areas by state and is part of Literature for a Land Ethic, a program sponsored by Milkweed Editions to educate, promote dialogue, and foster action on the critical environmental issues of our communities.

Abstract: This book was published in response to a congressional debate about acreage and boundaries for federally designated wilderness areas in Utah. The Utah delegation had called for only 1.8 million of 22 million acres of Utah wilderness to be designated "public lands." This bill would have undermined the 1964 Wilderness Act and opened up lands previously not designated for development, allowing gas pipelines, communication towers, and dams to be built. Essays include "Introduction: Bearing Witness" (T. H. Watkins); "In Praise of Emptiness" (Ann Weiler Walka); "Our Gardens, Our Canyons" (Stephen Trimble); "Decision Time" (Karen Shepherd); "Glen Canyon on the Colorado" (Richard Shelton); "Untouched Country" (Rick Bass); "Visionary Mammals" (Ellen Meloy); "Basin and Range" (John McPhee); "How Wonderful We Are" (Mark Strand); "Waiting on Wisdom" (Barry Lopez); "Bloodlines" (Terry Tempest Williams); "The Wingate and Time" (Charles Wilkinson); "A World

Not Lost" (Olive Ghiselin); "Vantage" (Brewster Ghiselin); "The Thigh Bone of a Mouse" (Ann Zwinger); "At Home in the World" (N. Scott Momaday); "A Redrock Place of the Heart" (Gary Paul Nabhan); "Sanity" (William Kittredge); "A Visit to Mom's" (Donald Snow); "A Tithe to the Wild" (Thomas J. Lyon); and "Wilderness Credo" (Margaret E. Murie).

A Sense of Belonging:
Education for Living Well in Community

Berry, Wendell. *What Are People For?* San Francisco: North Point Press, 1990.

Wendell Berry lives, farms, and writes in his native homeplace of Henry County, Kentucky. From his hillside, he ponders the sustainability of land and people on the land. *What Are People For?* is a collection of essays that examines the way we live within our culture and environment and the way we live with one another. Berry challenges us to recognize the long-term effects of what we do to our earth, our communities, and each other. He writes with insight on human nature, land use and abuse, and what it means to live well. Berry finds hope in the strength of communities and the power of rural life. In "The Work of Local Culture," he writes, "The renewal of the rural communities . . . would have to be a revival accomplished mainly by the community itself . . . from the inside by the ancient rule of neighborliness, by the love of precious things, and by the wish to be at home."

Abstract: These 22 essays highlight dysfunctional aspects of the relationship between people and the land. The first essay describes Berry's own well-intentioned, but ill-advised, attempts at building a pond on his farm, a project that ended up doing more harm than good. In another, he reviews a book about the life of Nate Shaw, a well-respected and successful Black farmer who was imprisoned in 1933 for taking a stand against sheriff deputies who had come to take away a neighbor's stock. Other essays relate the writings of authors such as Harry Caudill, Edward Abbey, and Wallace Stegner to the theme of a misguided society; address the relationship between Christianity and ecology; describe the problems of contemporary agricultural practices and an industrial economy that destroy the land and natural resources; address how education perpetuates a dysfunctional society by educating children to leave home and earn money while ignoring the themes of place and community; confront barriers to achieving harmony between nature and human economy; and look at our roles as stewards of the land. Berry also criticizes the rampant waste and pollution of society, questions the unqualified acceptance of new technologies, and objects to the fundamental economic structures that have destroyed rural culture and communities. Berry advocates decentralization, small-scale industries, diverse local economies, and personal actions that empower people to solve their own problems as opposed to the government's large-scale solutions to large-scale problems.

Peshkin, Alan. *Growing Up American: Schooling and the Survival of Community.* Chicago: University of Chicago Press, 1978; Prospect Heights, IL: Waveland Press, 1994.

Alan Peshkin was one of the first modern sociologists to point out the connection between school and community in small rural places. His chronicle of Mansfield (population 2,200) shows how growing up and educating young people in rural places is different from the same experiences in more crowded settings. The book's life comes from the interviews, in which people of Mansfield make sense of themselves and what matters to them. Particularly interesting are the voices of students describing what goes on in school and what it means to them. This is a great book for rural students to read and compare with their own experiences as an introduction to the study of community.

Abstract: Using the participant-observer technique, work began in Mansfield in August 1972 and continued for the next year and a half. The material strengthened the theory that the rural school and community are closely related; when the school is removed, the community is likely to disappear. Because this was an in-depth study of just one community and school, Peshkin took care not to generalize findings to rural communities across America; however, hundreds of rural communities will recognize striking similarities concerning the strong school-community relationship.

Theobald, Paul. *Teaching the Commons: Place, Pride and the Renewal of Community.* Boulder, CO: Westview Press, 1997.

Paul Theobald looks at history with the thought of "what if?" What if we had adopted the Greek understanding of community and civic involvement? What if we had continued the responsibilities of a Roman citizen? What if the commons had not been fenced? What would community mean then? He demonstrates how alternative historical paths could have led us to a far different present, one in which schools would operate very differently indeed. The final third of the book points a way toward the simultaneous renewal of rural schools and communities. It is written with a clear eye for the "peaks and valleys that come with this work." Theobald hopes to spark a populist campaign of people studying together, arguing with one another, and creating their own alternatives to the current wisdom about how the world works.

Abstract: This book addresses how rural schools can help promote the community and develop a community-oriented worldview. Theobald suggests rural schools should rekindle community allegiance and nurture the fulfillment that one finds in meeting community obligations. "The Creation of Community from a Historical Perspective" proposes that intradependence, cyclic time, and the avoidance of risk were once vital parts of the health and well-being of communities. These characteristics, though in severe decline, still linger in rural portions of the United States. The decline of these characteristics has coincided with the rise of an industrial worldview about what constitutes self, the economy, the proper role of government, and proper education to compete in a global economy. "Public Policy and the Subordination of Community" chronicles the historical developments that undermined the community and bolstered cultural infatuation with the individual. The decline of rural communities was caused by urban, commercialist interests acting under the guise of progress.

Greene, Melissa Fay. *Praying for Sheetrock: A Work of Nonfiction.* Reading, MA: Addison-Wesley, 1991; New York: Fawcett Books, 1992.

Greene tells the story of the political awakening of a tiny African American community on the seacoast of Georgia in the 1970s. This page-turner captures real human drama, comedy, and courage. The rich and varied stories are told by the people of McIntosh County with the intimacy of front-porch exchanges. It is about community, working together, and the lives of ordinary people moved to great deeds. Important things happen in a very little place. Greene discusses the end of the good-old-boy era, the Civil Rights movement, and what outsiders seem like to backwater Georgia.

Abstract: This book relates the downfall of a White sheriff and the subsequent political rise of a disabled Black boilermaker. Sheriff Tom Poppell was reelected every term until his death in 1979, completing the longest sheriff's dynasty in the history of Georgia. For 31 years, Poppell and his courthouse gang maintained the status quo by enforcing race, class, and gender distinctions. They shunned the modern industrial development that offered civil equality and higher wages. For years, African Americans, who were segregated in run-down shacks, came into town to work for the White community, which catered to tourists. Sheriff Poppell became rich through illegal businesses that ripped off tourists and sabotaged and looted wrecked trucks. Everyone in the state knew of the corruption, but no one would touch Poppell because of his entrenched authority. Ironically, Poppell was friends with many in the Black community. There was no snarling hatred, no overt abuse, and no police brutality. But that all changed in 1972, when a White police chief shot a Black man in the face because he annoyed him, evoking a response that was sudden, bitter, and communal. Thurnell Alston, a disabled boilermaker, organized the African American community by enlisting the services of young White lawyers from Brunswick. In 1978, Alston became the first Black elected to the county commission. Alston ensured that the commission was accountable with its funds and supported basic services that benefitted poor Blacks. In essence, Alston paved the way for the Black community to have a political voice in McIntosh County.

Verghese, Abraham. *My Own Country: A Doctor's Story of a Town and Its People in the Age of AIDS.* New York: Simon & Schuster, 1994; New York: Vintage Books, 1995.

Only urban romantics think rural America is protected from the ills afflicting the rest of society. Rural Americans know the problems of urban society are their problems as well, and solutions are sometimes complicated by the small stages on which events are played in rural places. AIDS presents the most recent of such dramas. Here we have AIDS in the Bible Belt. Verghese was the first doctor to write at book length about his experience with AIDS patients. He relates how the disease changed Johnson City, Tennessee, and altered his understanding of the community, his profession, and himself.

Abstract: The first AIDS patient appeared unexpectedly in Johnson City in 1985; within the next five years, Dr. Verghese had cared for eighty others. These stories illustrate the range of reactions to AIDS among patients, families, community members, and medical personnel. They also chronicle the doctor's personal journey as he becomes closely involved in his patients' lives and comes to grips with his own fears and unconscious beliefs about the disease.

Stack, Carol B. *Call to Home: African Americans Reclaim the Rural South.* New York: Basic Books, 1996; New York: HarperCollins, 1997.

Call to Home is the story of an amazing reverse migration. It is about a homecoming for African Americans, many of whom lived in the North for generations, returning to the American South to build real communities and set things right. Leaving apartments and houses in urban areas, African Americans have moved to brick houses on dusty back roads in small towns to start new lives as full citizens of the South. In this powerful and moving book, Stack tells us why and how they are succeeding.

Abstract: This book is based on research in rural areas of North and South Carolina, considered the top nonmetropolitan destinations in the South for African Americans. By 1975, the U.S. Census Bureau had released the first numbers suggesting an end to the exodus of Southern Blacks to cities of the North and West. By 1990, the South had regained more than 500,000 African Americans who had migrated north during the 1960s. As they returned to the South, children were often sent home first, either to be cared for by or to help care for grandparents. This book illustrates the hardships of starting over, facing poverty, and adapting to rural life. It also relates social and political successes, such as community action that resulted in day-care and youth programs.

Charney, Ruth Sidney. *Teaching Children to Care: Management in the Responsive Classroom.* Greenfield, MA: Northeast Foundation for Children, 1992.

This book is the next best thing to a very good friend. Charney analyzes the struggle of "placing the integrity of theory against the immediacy of the classroom" and willingly conveys what has happened in her classroom, even when it is a mess. Rooted in an affection for moral and ethical behavior, she helps her students create self-control and a sense of community in the classroom. Charney's concrete suggestions, formulated from years of classroom experience, are sure to inspire teachers at every level.

Abstract: This book is about managing a responsive classroom and teaching children to care. Chapters address goals of self-control and community; techniques of the first six weeks of school and their extension through the rest of the year; basic classroom rules and how children can be involved in their creation; a system of logical consequences for children's actions; problem-solving class meetings; a time-out procedure; children who engage in power struggles; problem solving with individuals and groups based on a teacher's ability to notice and reflect; the powerful link between words and actions; the use of specific language by children and teachers; different ways teachers can invoke authority, such as the Golden Rule, rules for safety and order, and personal rules; formation of "Clear Positives" or basic ideals; social arrangements and expectations; class and group expectations for learning content and procedures; individual expectations; and "critical contracts."

Wigginton, Eliot. *Sometimes a Shining Moment: The Foxfire Experience (Twenty Years Teaching in a High School Classroom).* Garden City, NY: Anchor Books, 1985; New York: Doubleday, 1986.

A classic, *Sometimes A Shining Moment* is actually two books in one. The first is the story of how Foxfire came to be. Unable to get high school English students interested in literature, Wigginton abandoned textbooks and set out on an unmapped journey of teaching communication skills through the study of local history and culture. The Foxfire legacy is well-known: a series of books written by students and published by a major publisher, a Broadway play, and a foundation. It is a fascinating story but not the most important part of the book. In the last section, Wigginton contemplates how teachers can make student learning more interesting and powerful by engaging in a study of their place. More than a "how-to manual," it also considers the "what" of education. It is about how teachers can help students find meaning in their lives, understand their community, and learn to live well in that place.

Abstract: In addition to the Foxfire story, this book discusses the role of the teacher; examines questions about power in the school; outlines overarching truths about teacher knowledge, the teacher-student relationship, discipline, and professional growth; and suggests educational goals that teachers should hold for their students. The first part details the activities entailed in a 12-week, project-based grammar and composition course.

Index to Place Value